## Bertolt Brecht: Bad Time For Poetry

'Brecht was that very rare phenomenon: a great
poet for whom poetry is an almost everyday
visitation and drawing of breath . . . there is no
doubt that the two great German poets of the
first half of this century were Rilke and Brecht.'

George Steiner, *The New Yorker*

'Of all the German-speaking writers of his
generation, Brecht alone has established himself
as a "classic", and not only in his own language
– across the political divisions – but
internationally . . . To me, Brecht's poetry is his
most durable and exemplary achievement.'

Michael Hamburger

Bertolt Brecht's reputation as a poet has for
many years been obscured by his achievements
in the theatre. This selection of his poems and
songs, including previously unpublished
material, offers the reader a fresh perspective on
one of this century's most influential writers. It
combines private and public poems from all
stages of an intense and turbulent life as well as
the most popular lyrics from plays such as
*The Threepenny Opera, Mother Courage* and
*Mahagonny*.

Bertolt Brecht by Caspar Neher

The inscription reads: 'Herewith Hydratopyranthropos, the water-fire man, who lived at Augsburg for one century, 1898–1998, a century of songs and machines. Greater than Mont Blanc, if not the Himalaya. A head of benevolence and integrity, always keeping a well-balanced mind; a friend to boys and girls, a terror to his enemies. To his right the globe, to his left a hostel for paupers and boozers; in the distance the Himalaya. A smiling moon, beneath it the lucid Atlantic sea. Presented [?] by Caspar Neher AD 1925.'

# Bertolt Brecht Bad Time For Poetry

Was it? Is it?

152 poems and songs

edited and introduced by
John Willett

Methuen

First published in Great Britain 1995
by Methuen London
an imprint of Reed International Books Ltd
Michelin House, 81 Fulham Road, London SW3 6RB
and Auckland, Melbourne, Singapore and Toronto
by arrangement with Suhrkamp Verlag, Frankfurt am Main

This edition, including introduction and notes,
copyright © 1995 by Methuen London
For full copyright notices in the original poems and songs
and in the translations see the last page of this book

Many of the poems in this selection were previously published in
Bertolt Brecht: *Poems 1913–1956* (Eyre Methuen, 1976; paperback
1981) and *Poems and Songs from the Plays* (Methuen London, 1990;
paperback 1992)

A CIP catalogue record for this book
is available from the British Library
ISBN 0 413 69050 4

Frontispiece: portrait of Bertolt Brecht by Caspar Neher from the
appendix to *Die Hauspostille*, courtesy of Staats- und Stadtbibliothek,
Augsburg

Typeset by Wilmaset Ltd, Birkenhead, Wirral
Printed and bound in Great Britain by
Cox & Wyman Ltd, Reading, Berkshire

# Contents

THE TRANSLATORS

Edith Anderson · W. H. Auden · Lee Baxendall ·
Derek Bowman · Martin Esslin · Michael Hamburger ·
Elisabeth Hauptmann · H. R. Hays · Nicholas Jacobs ·
Frank Jellinek · Lesley Lendrum ·
Christopher Middleton · Humphrey Milnes ·
Michael Morley · Patty Lee Parmalee ·
Naomi Replansky · Edith Roseveare ·
William Rowlinson · Stephen Spender · Martin Sutton ·
Antony Tatlow · John Willett

# Bad time for poetry?

Brecht died in 1956, when he was thought of above all as a radical playwright and theatre innovator whose works (like *The Threepenny Opera*) might contain some memorable songs. But right through his life he was a poet, even though it was only after 1970 that the range and variety of his poetry could be generally seen. That is to say, of course, his poetry in the original German. The English (and other) translation of the poems only gathered impetus later. And up to now we have had no easily accessible selection of them. Nor have songs and other poems been published together in a single volume.

He had lived through two world wars – the first as a schoolboy, medical student and short-term army recruit; the second as an exiled writer bitterly opposed to the government of his country – and he closely followed the disastrous events that led from the one war to the other. Then he returned to a defeated Germany to help clear up the mess, particularly the mess as he saw it in the theatre. He chose the Eastern, Communist-run half of that divided country, where he found considerable official support despite some basic cultural disagreements; his plays of the thirties and early forties, along with their realisation by the Ensemble which he founded, became influential right across the world.

So the first object of the present book is to offer a cross-section through the whole wide range of the poet's work: psalms, ballads, poems inspired by Kipling, Villon, Shelley; songs for various contexts; sonnets, epigrams, and poems in his own brand of irregular unrhymed verse. We want to give fresh readers a good sample of what Brecht is really about, incidentally reminding them that discussion of his character and love life is a very secondary matter. Here they can see how song and poetry relate; how new ideas and images enliven traditional forms; how exact, economical description of objects can be as exciting as the wildest rhetoric or passion.

Among them are a small number of poems or translations which have not been published before. Some are taken from the proposed sequel to the two Methuen/Minerva collections; others are translations that have been newly adjusted to their musical settings. The few editorial notes at the end refer mostly to these; for the rest the reader must turn to the notes in *Poems 1913–1956* and *Poems and Songs from the Plays*. He or she will find the relevant page or poem numbers in the detailed list of contents at the end of the book, which also gives indications of date, translator and composer of any notable musical setting for each of the 152 items.

Roughly two-thirds of the way through this book comes the poem which gives it its title. 'Bad time for poetry', says Brecht in 1939. It is spring and the apple tree is flowering; Prague is occupied by the German army; the Second World War is five months off. That was a bad time for humanity, certainly, although it would have been a much worse one if Hitler had been allowed to continue his conquests unopposed; and Brecht's particular conception of 'the dark times' had actually begun about a year earlier, when Hitler's annexation of Austria coincided with the worsening of the Soviet purges, in which three close associates of the poet would lose their lives.

But were those times in fact so bad for his poetry? Eighteen years ago, in the introduction to the main Methuen volume *Poems 1913– 1956*, we suggested that Brecht was 'all the time finding the words, the forms and the images for the disastrous history of Germany between the First World War and the aftermath of Stalin's death. More painfully (and in the long run more powerfully) than in any of his stage works, he was writing the tragedy of our time.' To those Europeans and Americans who themselves lived through a substantial part of the period, this still seems true, though Brecht's momentary rejection of rhyme – like his reluctance to write about the beauties of nature – was soon enough overcome. Even within the poems of that truly bad year we find prose 'Visions', sonnets, nature poems and epigrams. His keyboard still rattled.

So how far does his poetry remain valid today? Is our present time, with its freedom from major wars and its smiling 'have a nice day' attitude to life and politics, all that immune to the troubles that afflicted Germany when Brecht was at the height of his powers? One of the things that younger people have surely learned since Brecht's death is that the society which produced Hitler is a good deal less remote from our own than their parents and teachers used to believe. Poems of the 1920s and early 30s like 'The opium smoker', 'The unemployed', 'The song of the stimulating impact of cash', or the poems from the 'Reader for Those Who Live in Cities' still apply in our present world; and perhaps the realisation that they do so may put readers more on the lookout for the disastrous effects.

It was the Frankfurt philosopher Theodor Adorno – a fellow-exile for whom Brecht had little respect – who doubted whether literature could still be written after Auschwitz. In so far as Brecht's vision, like his language, was able to encompass even the camps, his poetry suggests otherwise. At the same time it gives the lie to those who, at the end of the Second World War, were lamenting the lack of 'war poets' such as had become recognised in England during and after the First. Of course Brecht saw war from a different, entirely non-combatant angle, and had seen it coming for several years. And even after 1945 he was apprehensive about its continuation, in one form or another, as a war of capitalism against Soviet Russia. But his sensitivity to its symptoms was extraordinary, and all the more so because his reactions were expressed in such intelligible forms and with such striking clarity.

Is this what is meant by 'post-modern' writing? In only one aspect is Brecht's poetry formally innovative: his particular use of what he termed 'rhymeless verse with irregular rhythms', where there is a tiny pause at the end of each line (roughly equivalent to a comma) when the poet says 'wait for it', provoking the reader to note the next word or turn of thought. But the resulting structure is more deliberate than is sometimes supposed – it is not absolute *vers libre* – and otherwise his choice of forms is largely traditional. What is new is the use which he makes of them: the ideas and images with which they are packed. So yes, it was a bad time for poetry. But the result was poetry for a bad time. And much the same is true of the bad time which our societies continue to experience today. This is a book which can be read through or thumbed at random. Either way it remains alive.

John Willett
Autumn 1994

Who built Thebes of the seven gates?
In the books you will find the names of kings.
Did the kings haul up the lumps of rock?
And Babylon, many times demolished
Who raised it up so many times? In what houses
Of gold-glittering Lima did the builders live?
Where, the evening that the Wall of China was finished
Did the masons go? Great Rome
Is full of triumphal arches. Who erected them? Over whom
Did the Caesars triumph? Had Byzantium, much praised in
      song
Only palaces for its inhabitants? Even in fabled Atlantis
The night the ocean engulfed it
The drowning still bawled for their slaves.

The young Alexander conquered India.
Was he alone?
Caesar beat the Gauls.
Did he not have even a cook with him?

Philip of Spain wept when his armada
Went down. Was he the only one to weep?
Frederick the Second won the Seven Years' War. Who
Else won it?

Every page a victory.
Who cooked the feast for the victors?
Every ten years a great man.
Who paid the bill?

So many reports.
So many questions.

## MY AUDIENCE

The other day I met my audience.
In a dusty street
He gripped a pneumatic drill in his fists.
For a second
He looked up. Rapidly I set up my theatre
Between the houses. He
Looked expectant.

In the pub
I met him again. He was standing at the bar.
Grimy with sweat, he was drinking. In his fist
A thick sandwich. Rapidly I set up my theatre. He
Looked astonished.

Today
I brought it off again. Outside the station
With brass bands and rifle butts I saw him
Being herded off to war.
In the midst of the crowd
I set up my theatre. Over his shoulder
He looked back
And nodded.


## OF ALL THE WORKS OF MAN

Of all the works of man I like best
Those which have been used.
The copper pots with their dents and flattened edges
The knives and forks whose wooden handles
Have been worn away by many hands: such forms
Seemed to me the noblest. So too the flagstones round old
      houses
Trodden by many feet, ground down

And with tufts of grass growing between them: these
Are happy works.

Absorbed into the service of the many
Frequently altered, they improve their shape, grow precious
Because so often appreciated.
Even broken pieces of sculpture
With their hands lopped off, are dear to me. They too
Were alive for me. They were dropped, yet they were
      carried.
They were knocked down, yet they never stood too high
Half ruined buildings once again take on
The look of buildings waiting to be finished
Generously planned: their fine proportions
Can already be guessed at, but they still
Need our understanding. At the same time
They have already served, indeed have already been
      overcome. All this
Delights me.

YEARS AGO WHEN I

Years ago when I was studying the ways of the Chicago
      Wheat Exchange
I suddenly grasped how they managed the whole world's
      wheat there
And yet I did not grasp it either and lowered the book
I knew at once: you've run
Into bad trouble.

There was no feeling of enmity in me and it was not the
      injustice
Frightened me, only the thought that
Their way of going about it won't do
Filled me completely.

These people, I saw, lived by the harm
Which they did, not by the good.
This was a situation, I saw, that could only be maintained
By crime, as being too bad for most people.
In this way every
Achievement of reason, invention or discovery
Must lead only to still greater wretchedness.

Such and suchlike I thought at that moment
Far from anger or lamenting, as I lowered the book
With its description of the Chicago wheat market and
            exchange.

Much trouble and tribulation
Awaited me.


## THE PLAY IS OVER

The play is over. The performance committed. Slowly
The theatre, a sagging intestine, empties. In the dressing
            rooms
The nimble salesmen of hotchpotch mimicry, of rancid
            rhetoric
Wash off make-up and sweat. At last
The lights go down which showed up the miserable
Botched job; twilight falls on the
Lovely nothingness of the misused stage. In the empty
Still mildly smelly auditorium sits the honest
Playwright, unappeased, and does his best
To remember.

## LEGEND OF THE DEAD SOLDIER

I

And when the war reached its final spring
With no hint of a pause for breath
The soldier did the logical thing
And died a hero's death.

2

The war however was far from done
And the Kaiser thought it a crime
That his soldier should be dead and gone
Before the proper time.

3

The summer spread over the makeshift graves
And the soldier lay ignored
Until one night there came an offi-
cial army medical board.

4

The board went out to the cemetery
With consecrated spade
And dug up what was left of him
For next day's sick parade.

5

Their doctor inspected what they'd found
Or as much as he thought would serve
And gave his report: 'He's medically sound
He's merely lost his nerve.'

6

Straightway they took the soldier off.
The night was soft and warm.
If you hadn't a helmet you could see
The stars you saw at home.

7
They filled him up with a fiery schnapps
To spark his sluggish heart
And shoved two nurses into his arms
And a half-naked tart.

8
He's stinking so strongly of decay
That a priest limps on before
Swinging a censer on his way
That he may stink no more.

9
In front the band with oompah-pah
Intones a rousing march.
The soldier does like the manual says
And flicks his legs from his arse.

10
Their arms about him, keeping pace
Two kind first-aid men go
Or else he might fall in the shit on his face
And that would never do.

11
They daubed his shroud with the black-white-red
Of the old imperial flag
Whose garish colours obscured the mud
On that blood-bespattered rag.

12
Up front a gent in a morning suit
And stuffed-out shirt marched too:
A German determined to do his dut-
y as Germans always do.

13
So see them now as, oompah-pah
Along the roads they go
And the soldier goes whirling along with them
Like a flake in the driving snow.

14
The dogs cry out and the horses prance
The rats squeal on the land:
They're damned if they're going to belong to France
It's more than flesh can stand.

15
And when they pass through a village all
The women are moved to tears.
The trees bow low, the moon shines full
And the whole lot gives three cheers.

16
With oompah-pah and cheerio
And tart and dog and priest
And right in the middle the soldier himself
Like some poor drunken beast.

17
And when they pass through a village perhaps
It happens he disappears
For such a crowd's come to join the chaps
With oompah and three cheers.

18
In all that dancing, yelling crowd
He disappeared from view.
You could only see him from overhead
Which only stars can do.

19
The stars won't always be up there
The dawn is turning red.
But the soldier goes off to a hero's death
Just like the manual said.


THE FIRST PSALM

1 How terrifying it is in the night, the convex face of the black land!

2 Above the world are the clouds, they belong to the world. Above the clouds there is nothing.

3 The solitary tree in the stony field must be feeling it is all in vain. It has never seen a tree. There are no trees.

4 I keep on thinking we are not observed. The leprosy of the sole star in the night before it goes under!

5 The warm wind is still trying to connect things, the Catholic.

6 I am very much an isolated case. I have no patience. Our poor brother Godrewardyou said of the world: it doesn't count.

7 We are travelling at high speed towards a star in the Milky Way. There is a great calm in the earth's face. My heart beats too fast. Otherwise all is well.

## THE SECOND PSALM

1 Under a flesh-coloured sun that brightens the eastern sky four breaths after midnight, under a heap of wind that covers them in gusts as with shrouds, the meadows from Füssen to Passau spread their lust-for-life propaganda.

2 From time to time the trains full of milk and passengers cleave the wheatfield oceans; but around the thunderers the air stands still, the light between the great petrifacts, the noon over the motionless fields.

3 The figures in the fields, brown-chested monsters, wicked looking, work with slow movements for the pale-faces in the petrifacts, as laid down in the documents.

4 For God created the earth that it might bring bread, and gave us those with brown chests that this might enter our stomachs, mixed with the milk from the cows which he created. But what is the wind for, glorious in the tree tops?

5 The wind makes the clouds, that there may be rain on the ploughland, that bread may come. Let us now make children out of our lusts, for the bread, that it may be devoured.

6 This is summer. Scarlet winds excite the plains, the smells at the end of June grow boundless. Vast visions of teeth-gnashing naked men travel at great heights southward.

7 In the cottages the light of the nights is like salmon. The resurrection of the flesh is being celebrated.

## THE FOURTH PSALM

1 What do people still expect of me?
I have played all the patiences, spat out all the kirsch
Stuffed all the books into the stove
Loved all the women till they stank like Leviathan.
Truly I am a great saint, my ear is so rotten it will soon drop
off.
So why is there no peace? Why do the people stand in the
yard like rubbish bins – waiting for something to be put into
them?
I have made it plain it is no use any more to expect the Song
of Songs from me.
I have set the police on the buyers.
Whoever it is you are looking for, it is not me.

2 I am the most practical of all my brothers –
And it all starts in *my* head!
My brothers were cruel, I am the cruellest
And it is *I* who weep at night!

3 When the tables of the law broke, so did all vices.
Even sleeping with one's sister is no fun any more.
Murder is too much trouble for many
Writing poems is too common
Since everything is too uncertain
Many prefer to tell the truth
Being ignorant of the danger.
The courtesans pickle meat for the winter
And the devil no longer carries away his best people.

## SONG ABOUT MY MOTHER

1 I no longer remember her face as it was before her pains began. Wearily, she pushed the black hair back from her forehead, which was bony, I can still see her hand as she does it.

2 Twenty winters had threatened her, her sufferings were legion, death was ashamed to approach her. Then she died, and they discovered that her body was like a child's.

3 She grew up in the forest.

4 She died among faces which had looked so long at her dying that they had grown hard. One forgave her for suffering, but she was wandering among those faces before she collapsed.

5 There are many who leave us without our detaining them. We have said all there is to say, there is nothing more between them and us, our faces hardened as we parted. But we did not say the important things, but saved on essentials.

6 Oh why do we not say the important things, it would be so easy, and we are damned because we do not. Easy words, they were, pressing against our teeth; they fell out as we laughed, and now they choke us.

7 Now my mother has died, yesterday towards evening, on the First of May. One won't be able to claw her up out again with one's fingernails.

## BALLAD OF THE PIRATES

### 1

Frantic with brandy from their plunder
Drenched in the blackness of the gale
Splintered by frost and stunned by thunder
Hemmed in the crows-nest, ghostly pale
Scorched by the sun through tattered shirt
(The winter sun kept them alive)
Amid starvation, sickness, dirt
So sang the remnant that survived:
   Oh heavenly sky of streaming blue!
   Enormous wind, the sails blow free!
   Let wind and heavens go hang! But oh
   Sweet Mary, let us keep the sea!

### 2

No waving fields with gentle breezes
Or dockside bar with raucous band
No dance hall warm with gin and kisses
No gambling hell kept them on land.
They very quickly tired of fighting
By midnight girls began to pall:
Their rotten hulk seemed more inviting
That ship without a flag at all.
   Oh heavenly sky of streaming blue!
   Enormous wind, the sails blow free!
   Let wind and heavens go hang! But oh
   Sweet Mary, let us keep the sea!

### 3

Riddled with rats, its bilges oozing
With pestilence and puke and piss
They swear by her when they're out boozing
And cherish her just as she is.
In storms they'll reckon their position
Lashed to the halyards by their hair:

They'd go to heaven on one condition –
That she can find a mooring there.
   Oh heavenly sky of streaming blue!
   Enormous wind, the sails blow free!
   Let wind and heavens go hang! But oh
   Sweet Mary, let us keep the sea!

4
They loot their wine and belch with pleasure
While bales of silk and bars of gold
And precious stones and other treasure
Weigh down the rat-infested hold.
To grace their limbs, all hard and shrunken
Sacked junks yield vari-coloured stuffs
Till out their knives come in some drunken
Quarrel about a pair of cuffs.
   Oh heavenly sky of streaming blue!
   Enormous wind, the sails blow free!
   Let wind and heavens go hang! But oh
   Sweet Mary, let us keep the sea!

5
They murder coldly and detachedly
Whatever comes across their path
They throttle gullets as relaxedly
As fling a rope up to the mast.
At wakes they fall upon the liquor
Then stagger overboard and drown
While the remainder give a snigger
And wave a toe as they go down.
   Oh heavenly sky of streaming blue!
   Enormous wind, the sails blow free!
   Let wind and heavens go hang! But oh
   Sweet Mary, let us keep the sea!

6

Across a violet horizon
Caught in the ice by pale moonlight
On pitch-black nights when mist is rising
And half the ship is lost from sight
They lurk like wolves between the hatches
And murder for the fun of it
And sing to keep warm in their watches
Like children drumming as they shit.
    Oh heavenly sky of streaming blue!
    Enormous wind, the sails blow free!
    Let wind and heavens go hang! But oh
    Sweet Mary, let us keep the sea!


7

They take their hairy bellies with them
To stuff with food on foreign ships
Then stretch them out in sweet oblivion
Athwart the foreign women's hips.
In gentle winds, in blue unbounded
Like noble beasts they graze and play
And often seven bulls have mounted
Some foreign girl they've made their prey.
    Oh heavenly sky of streaming blue!
    Enormous wind, the sails blow free!
    Let wind and heavens go hang! But oh
    Sweet Mary, let us keep the sea!


8

Once you have danced till you're exhausted
And boozed until your belly sags
Though sun and moon unite their forces –
Your appetite for fighting flags.
Brilliant with stars, the night will shake them
While music plays, in gentle ease
And wind will fill their sails and take them
To other, undiscovered seas.

Oh heavenly sky of streaming blue!
Enormous wind, the sails blow free!
Let wind and heavens go hang! But oh
Sweet Mary, let us keep the sea!

9
But then upon an April evening
Without a star by which to steer
The placid ocean, softly heaving
Decides that they must disappear.
The boundless sky they love is hiding
The stars in smoke that shrouds their sight
While their beloved winds are sliding
The clouds towards the gentle light.

Oh heavenly sky of streaming blue!
Enormous wind, the sails blow free!
Let wind and heavens go hang! But oh
Sweet Mary, let us keep the sea!

10
At first they're fanned by playful breezes
Into the night they mustn't miss
The velvet sky smiles once, then closes
Its hatches on the black abyss.
Once more they feel the kindly ocean
Watching beside them on their way
The wind then lulls them with its motion
And kills them all by break of day.

Oh heavenly sky of streaming blue!
Enormous wind, the sails blow free!
Let wind and heavens go hang! But oh
Sweet Mary, let us keep the sea!

11
Once more the final wave is tossing
The cursed vessel to the sky
When suddenly it clears, disclosing

The mighty reef on which they lie.
And, at the last, a strange impression
While rigging screams and storm winds howl
Of voices hurtling to perdition
Yet once more singing, louder still:
　　Oh heavenly sky of streaming blue!
　　Enormous wind, the sails blow free!
　　Let wind and heavens go hang! But oh
　　Sweet Mary, let us keep the sea!


OF FRANÇOIS VILLON

I
François Villon was a poor man's son
The cool breeze sang his only lullaby.
All through his youth in sleet and wind the one
Thing beautiful around was endless sky.
　　François Villon, who never had a bed to lie in
　　Found soon enough cool wind was satisfying.

2
With bruised backside and bleeding feet, he found
Stones are keener than rock to lacerate.
He soon learned to cast stones at those around
And, once he'd skinned them all, to celebrate.
　　And if it stretched to something fortifying
　　He soon enough found stretching satisfying.

3
God's table was denied to him for life
So Heaven's blessed gifts he could not get.
His fate it was to stab men with his knife
And stick his neck into the traps they set.
　　So let them kiss his arse while he was trying
　　To eat some food that he found satisfying.

4

He got no glimpse of Heaven's sweet rewards
Policemen broke his pride with their big hands
Yet he too was a child of our dear Lord's –
Long time he rode through wind and rain towards
Where his only reward, the gibbet, stands.

5

François Villon was never caught, but died
Concealed among some bushes, dodging gaol –
His ribald soul however will abide
Deathless as this my song which cannot stale.
   And when he lay, poor wretch, stretched out there dying
   He found this stretching too was satisfying.

BALLAD OF MAZEPPA

1

They took him and tied him with rope to his stallion
He was bound on his back to the back of his beast
In the darkening evening they drove him out quickly
With a whinnying wild shriek as his steed was released.

2

They tied him so tight that the man's senseless struggle
Inflamed his horse in a frenzy of pain
The man could see only the heavens above him
Ever darker, ever wider, beyond wind and rain.

3

Blind and despairing like a woman's devotion
The beast strode away from pursuit, till the thud
Of its hooves made the rope bite tighter and deeper
Into the body awash now with blood.

4
The wings of strange birds filled the heavens each evening;
The soaring of vultures, the hovering crow
Silently, darkly, the multitude followed
The sound of the galloping gasping below.


5
His platter of flesh carried him onward
Away to the point of endless departure
Three days of wildly whinnying shrieking
While heaven grew darker, then lighter, then darker.


6
For three days frantically faster and faster
Three times eternity passed on that ride
As heaven grew darker, then lighter, then darker
And ever extending immeasurably wide.


7
Suspended in flight between heaven and pasture
For three long days he lies stretched out to die
Yet he lives, as the crow and the vultures fly after
And watch for his corpse as it speeds swiftly by.


8
For three days he rode, with his ropes ever tightening
Green were the heavens and brown was the grass!
Above him the carrion birds wheeling and fighting
As the horse and its living-dead rider swept past!


9
And when he rode faster, they followed him eagerly
And when he screamed louder, they screamed with him
        too.
Darkening the sun and obscuring the starlight
Drawn on by the galloping gasping, they flew.

10

Three days, then the whole confusion is settled:
Earth grants its silence, the heavens their peace.
A man rode out with his sole possessions:
With the earth and his horse, with patience and silence
And those wings in the heavens that await his decease

11

Three days he had ridden through morning and evening
Till he reached the age where all pain is suppressed
And then he passed into the great haven of safety
Dead tired he rode on into infinite rest.

## BALLAD OF THE GIRL AND THE SOLDIER

The guns blaze away, and the bay'nit'll slay
And the water can't hardly be colder.
What's the answer to ice? 'Keep off!''s my advice.
That's what the girl told the soldier.
Next thing the soldier, wiv' a round up the spout
Hears the band playing and gives a great shout:
Why, it's marching what makes you a soldier!
So it's down to the south, and then northwards once more;
See him catching that bay'nit in his naked paw!
That's what his comrades done told her.

Oh, do not despise the advice of the wise
Learn wisdom from those that are older
And don't try for things that are out of your reach –
That's what the girl told the soldier.
Next thing the soldier, his bay'nit in place
Wades into the river and laughs in her face
Though the water comes up to his shoulder.
When the shingle roof glints in the light o' the moon
We'll be wiv' you again, not a moment too soon!
That's what his comrades done told her.

You'll go out like a light! And the sun'll take flight
For your courage just makes us feel colder.
Oh, that vanishing light! May God see that it's right! –
That's what the girl told the soldier.
Next thing the soldier, his bay'nit in place
Was caught by the current and went down without trace
And the water could hardly be colder.
Then the shingle roof froze in the light o' the moon
As both soldier and ice drifted down to their doom –
And d'you know what his comrades done told her?

He went out like a light. And the sunshine took flight
For his courage just made 'em feel colder.
Oh, do not despise the advice of the wise!
That's what the girl told the soldier.


THOSE DAYS OF MY YOUTH

Those days of my youth! Let me remember
(Only note how fast the memory goes).
Flimsy shadows. Walls with white distemper.
Nickelodeon *couleur de rose*.

Apple-clear the ponds where we went carping
Sinuous waters, buoyant greedy guts
Then at night the bowler-hatted larking
All of us in raspberry-coloured shirts.

Oh the harsh snarl of guitar strings roaring!
Heavenly distensions of our throats!
Trousers stiff with dirt and love! Such whoring!
Long green slimy nights: we were like stoats.

Lounging sleepily beneath the willows
Oh tobacco, apple-green sky above!

Flying like pigeons drunk on kirsch, poor fellows –
Ending limper than a worn-out glove.

Tender joint of lamb in fresh starched linen
Watch out, the good shepherd's on his way!
You may safely graze, and fill the skin in
Which your red heart sits, soon to decay.

## AN INSCRIPTION TOUCHES OFF
## SENTIMENTAL MEMORIES

### 1

Among those yellowed sheets that mattered once to me
(You drink, then read; it's better when you're pissed)
A photograph. Inscribed on which I see
The words PURE, LUCID, NASTY, through a mist.

### 2

She always used to wash with almond soap
The small rough towel was hers as well
And the Tokay recipe and the Javanese pipe
To cover up love's smell.

### 3

She took it seriously. She didn't float. She was thoughtful.
Art, in her view, demanded sacrifice.
She loved love, not her lover; no one could pull
The wool over her eyes.

### 4

She laughed, passiveness put up her back
As for her head, that was screwed on all right
She had a cold shoulder, and the knack:
Thinking of it I start to sweat with fright.

5
That was her. My God, I wish I had
An inscription like that on my tombstone: Here lies B.B.
PURE, LUCID, NASTY.
I'd sleep all right with that on top of me.


REMEMBERING MARIE A.

It was a day in that blue month September
Silent beneath a plum tree's slender shade
I held her there, my love so pale and silent
As if she were a dream that must not fade.
Above us in the shining summer heaven
There was a cloud my eyes dwelt long upon
It was quite white and very high above us
Then I looked up, and found that it had gone.

And since that day so many moons, in silence
Have swum across the sky and gone below.
The plum trees surely have been chopped for firewood
And if you ask, how does that love seem now?
I must admit: I really can't remember
And yet I know what you are trying to say.
But what her face was like I know no longer
I only know: I kissed it on that day.

As for the kiss, I'd long ago forgot it
But for the cloud that floated in the sky
I know that still, and shall for ever know it
It was quite white and moved in very high.
It may be that the plum trees still are blooming
That woman's seventh child may now be there
And yet that cloud had only bloomed for moments
When I looked up, it vanished on the air.

THE SHIP

1

Through the clear seas of countless oceans swimming
With sharks as escorts under red moons skimming
I tossed and shed direction, cast off gravity.
My timbers rotting and my sails in tatters
My ropes decaying in the salty waters
My horizon grew remoter, paler too my sky.


2

Since it turned paler and the remote horizon
Left me abandoned in my watery prison
I knew I must go down, and understood.
Once I had realised that there's no resistance
These seas must put an end to my existence
I let the waters take me where they would.


3

And the waters came, and swept vast numbers
Of creatures through me, so that in my timbers
Creature befriended creature in the gloom.
Once the sky fell through the rotting hatches
And they knew each other in the watches
And the sharks inside me felt at home.


4

Three moons passed, I filled with floating seaweeds
Which clutched my wood and greened across my bulkheads
Until my face told yet another tale.
Green and groaning deep below my middle
Slowly I moved, suffering but little
Weighed down by weed and moon, by shark and whale.

5

To gulls and seaweed I was a kind of haven
Not to be blamed because I failed to save them.
How slow and full I shall be as I drown
Now, eight moons gone, the waters spurting quickly
Through all my flanks, my face grows yet more sickly.
And I pray that I may soon go down.

6

*Unknown fishermen saw something nearing*
*Which as it neared seemed to be disappearing.*
*Was it an island? Or a raft passed by?*
*Something moved, agleam with seagulls' spatter*
*Loaded with moon and corpses, weed and water*
*Silent and stout towards the washed-out sky.*

OF POOR B.B.
(*early version*)

1

I, Bertolt Brecht, came out of the black forests.
My mother moved me into the cities while I lay
Inside her body. But it must be that the forests
Were inside me also and there to stay.

2

In the asphalt city I'm at home. For many years now
Provided with every unction and sacrament:
Between newspapers, tobacco and brandy
To the end mistrustful, lazy and content.

3

But in those deal bedsteads always I felt cold
And worst of all was the night.
Of all the bedrooms that I occupied
Not one became a home or seemed right.

4
By night the black forests are full of disquiet.
Amid the branchwork, it could be, animals cry and cough.
The great spruces are busy doing all sorts of things:
Ugh, to think who it is the forest's pale sky lets drowse off!

5
In the grey light before morning the spruces piss
And their vermin raise their twitter and cheep.
At that hour I drain my brandy glass, then throw
The cigar butt away and worriedly fall asleep.

6
For at times in the sight of many I play the guitar
And don't understand myself well and am fairly alone.
They lap up the coarse words. They're animals different
        from me.
But I lie there and in my back can still feel a stone.

7
Maybe, I think, I'm hung up on paper and women
And never again from the asphalt city I shall break loose.
Yet high above the roofs there's a pale forest sky all for me
And a black silence inside me, an uproar of spruce.

8
Whether I drink or not, when I see the black forests
Under my skin I'm good, beyond blame or blow –
I, Bertolt Brecht, carried off to the asphalt cities
From the black forests inside my mother long ago.

ALABAMA SONG

1

Oh, show us the way to the next whisky-bar
Oh, don't ask why, oh, don't ask why
For we must find the next whisky-bar
For if we don't find the next whisky-bar
I tell you we must die! I tell you we must die!
   Oh! Moon of Alabama
   We now must say goodbye
   We've lost our good old mamma
   And must have whisky
   Oh! You know why.

2

Oh, show us the way to the next pretty girl
Oh, don't ask why, oh, don't ask why
For we must find the next pretty girl
For if we don't find the next pretty girl
I tell you we must die! I tell you we must die!
   Oh! Moon of Alabama
   We now must say goodbye
   We've lost our good old mamma
   And must have a girl
   Oh! You know why.

3

Oh, show us the way to the next little dollar
Oh, don't ask why, oh, don't ask why
For we must find the next little dollar
For if we don't find the next little dollar
I tell you we must die! I tell you we must die!
   Oh! Moon of Alabama
   We now must say goodbye
   We've lost our good old mamma
   And must have dollars
   Oh! You know why.

MAHAGONNY SONG NO. I

Off to Mahagonny!
The air is cool and fresh.
There's horses there and poker dice
Whisky and women's flesh.
   Cleaner, greener
   Moon of Alabama
   Guide us in!
   Here we come with stacks of notes
   Underneath our overcoats
   For a great big welcome
   From your stupid empty grin.

Off to Mahagonny!
The wind is in the east
There's prime selected sirloin steak
And neither king nor priest.
   Cleaner, greener
   Moon of Alabama
   Guide us in!
   Here we come with stacks of notes
   Underneath our overcoats
   For a great big welcome
   From your stupid empty grin.

Off to Mahagonny!
It's time we went on board.
The over syph-syph-syphilised
Can go there to get cured.
   Cleaner, greener
   Moon of Alabama
   Guide us in!
   Here we come with stacks of notes
   Underneath our overcoats
   For a great big welcome
   From your stupid empty grin.

MAHAGONNY SONG NO. 3

One gloomy morning as we sat
Sipping our whisky
God came to Mahagonny
God came to Mahagonny.
Sipping our whisky
We caught sight of God in Mahagonny.


1
All you spongers mopping
Up My yearly bounty of good rye
Didn't think you'd ever see Me drop in
Shall I find you've drunk the whole place dry?
Looks were exchanged by the men of Mahagonny.
Yes, answered back the men of Mahagonny.
  One gloomy morning as we sat
  Sipping our whisky
  God came to Mahagonny
  God came to Mahagonny.
  Sipping our whisky
  We caught sight of God in Mahagonny.


2
Was it Friday night I heard you joking?
I was watching Mary Weeman then
Silent as a sprat, in salt seas soaking:
Will she ever dry out, gentlemen?
Looks were exchanged by the men of Mahagonny.
Yes, answered back the men of Mahagonny.
  One gloomy morning as we sat
  Sipping our whisky
  God came to Mahagonny
  God came to Mahagonny.
  Sipping our whisky
  We caught sight of God in Mahagonny.

3
What are those cartridge-cases?
Did you shoot My preacher good and true?
I can't stand your raddled boozer's faces.
Must I share My heavenly home with you?
Looks were exchanged by the men of Mahagonny.
Yes, answered back the men of Mahagonny.
   One gloomy morning as we sat
   Sipping our whisky
   God came to Mahagonny
   God came to Mahagonny.
   Sipping our whisky
   We caught sight of God in Mahagonny.


4
You can all go to hell now
Stuff your wet cigar-butts up your bum!
There's a hell for you to go to, fellows
Down to My black hell, you filthy scum!
Looks were exchanged by the men of Mahagonny.
Yes, answered back the men of Mahagonny.
   One gloomy morning as we sat
   Sipping our whisky
   You'll come to Mahagonny
   You'll come to Mahagonny.
   Sipping our whisky
   While you sort out Mahagonny.


5
So let nobody budge now!
All out on strike! We shall never
Go to hell, though Your wild horses drag us:
*For, You see, we've been in hell for ever.*
God got a look from the men of Mahagonny.
No, answered back the men of Mahagonny.

BENARES SONG

1

There is no whisky in this town
There is no bar to sit us down
Oh!
Where is the telephone?
Is here no telephone?
Oh, sir, God damn it:
No!
    Let's go to Benares
    Where the bars are plenty
    Let's go to Benares!
    Jenny, let us go.

2

There is no money in this town
The whole economy has broken down
Oh!
Where is the telephone?
Is here no telephone?
Oh, sir, God damn it:
No!
    Let's go to Benares
    Where there's money plenty
    Let's go to Benares!
    Jenny, let us go.

3

There is no fun on this old star
There is no door for us ajar
Oh!
Where is the telephone?
Is here no telephone?
Oh, sir, God damn it:
No!

Worst of all, Benares
Is said to have perished in an earthquake!
Oh! our good Benares!
Oh, where shall we go!
Worst of all, Benares
Is said to have been punished in an earthquake!
Oh! our good Benares!
Oh! where shall we go!

## DISCOVERY ABOUT A YOUNG WOMAN

Next day's subdued farewell: she standing there
Cool on the threshold, coolly looked at too
When I observed a grey strand in her hair
And found I could not bring myself to go.

Silent I took her breast, and when she wondered
Why I, who'd been her guest that night in bed
Was not prepared to leave as we had said
I looked her straight between the eyes and answered:

It's only one more night that I'll be staying
But use your time; the fact is, you've provoked me
Standing poised on the threshold in that way.

And let us speed up what we've got to say
For both of us forgot that you're decaying.
With that my voice gave out, and longing choked me.

## THE OPIUM SMOKER

A girl who smokes the black smoke of the evening
You know is vowed to nothingness in future.
There's nothing more can raise her up or hurt her
And two-thirds of the time she won't be living.

She can dispense with courage; she looks dreadful
(She and her hair are very nearly through)
And when she sees herself she'll wonder who
On earth that was: she's terribly forgetful.

The smoke invades her blood and fogs her wits
And so she sleeps alone: the soil is closest.
She's on the thinnest trip of her existence.

It's only others know she still exists
(She's ready for whatever won't be noticed)
She finds man's best friend, drugs, of some assistance.


## COW FEEDING

Her broad chest laid against the manger railing
She feeds. Just watch that hay! She does not gulp
But mashes it awhile, the ends still trailing
Then munches carefully until it's pulp.

Her body's stout, her ancient eye is bleary
Inured to wickedness, she chews with caution.
The years have made her see things in proportion
She's not surprised now at your interfering.

And while she gets the hay down someone
Is milking her. Patient, without a sound
She lets his hand go tweaking at her teats.

She knows that hand, and doesn't turn around
She'd sooner not know what is going on
But takes advantage of the evening mood, and shits.

### SONNET ON A NEW EDITION OF FRANÇOIS VILLON

Once more the fading letters come up clear
In this new version of his Testament
Where he doles out his lumps of excrement –
Will all who want a piece please answer 'Here!'?

Where is the snot you spat as he walked past?
Where is the man you told to stuff himself?
His verse has lasted longest on the shelf
But how much longer is it going to last?

Here, for the price of fifty cigarettes
You buy another chance to read it through
(And so to find out what he thought of you . . .)

It's sour but cheap; you pay three marks for it
And what a lucky dip the buyer gets!
I for my own part fished out quite a bit . . .


### ON DANTE'S POEMS TO BEATRICE

Even today, above the dusty vault
In which she lies, whom he could never have
Although he dogged her footsteps like a slave
Her name's enough to bring us to a halt.

For he ensured that we should not forget her
Writing such splendid verse to her as made
Us listen to the compliments he paid
Convinced that no one ever put it better.

Dear me, what an abuse he started then
By praising in a manner so arresting
What he had only looked at without testing!

Since he made poems out of glimpses, men
Have seen what looks nice in its street attire
And stays bone-dry, as something to desire.

## ON SHAKESPEARE'S PLAY *HAMLET*

Here is the body, puffy and inert
Where we can trace the virus of the mind.
How lost he seems among his steel-clad kind
This introspective sponger in a shirt.

Till they bring drums to wake him up again
As Fortinbras and all the fools he's found
March off to battle for that patch of ground
'Which is not tomb enough . . . to hide the slain'.

At that his too, too solid flesh sees red.
He feels he's hesitated long enough.
It's time to turn to (bloody) deeds instead.

So we nod grimly when the play is done
And they pronounce that he was of the stuff
To prove 'most royally', 'had he been put on'.

COVER YOUR TRACKS

Part from your friends at the station
Enter the city in the morning with your coat buttoned up
Look for a room, and when your friend knocks:
Do not, o do not, open the door
But
Cover your tracks.

If you meet your parents in Hamburg or elsewhere
Pass them like strangers, turn the corner, don't recognise
   them
Pull the hat they gave you over your face, and
Do not, o do not, show your face
But
Cover your tracks.

Eat the meat that's there. Don't stint yourself.
Go into any house when it rains and sit on any chair that's
   in it
But don't sit long. And don't forget your hat.
I tell you:
Cover your tracks.

Whatever you say, don't say it twice
If you find your ideas in anyone else, disown them.
The man who hasn't signed anything, who has left no
   picture
Who was not there, who said nothing:
How can they catch him?
Cover your tracks.

See when you come to think of dying
That no gravestone stands and betrays where you lie
With a clear inscription to denounce you
And the year of your death to give you away.

Once again:
Cover your tracks.

(That is what they taught me.)

## I'M DIRT

I'm dirt. From myself
I can demand nothing but
Weakness, treachery and degradation
Then one day I notice
It's getting better; the wind
Fills my sails; my time has come, I can
Become better than dirt –
I began at once.

Because I was dirt I noticed
When I'm drunk I simply
Lie down and have no idea
Who is messing me about; now I don't drink any more –
I gave it up at once.

Unfortunately
Just in order to keep alive, I had to do
Much that harmed me; I've
Wolfed down poison enough
To kill four carthorses, but
What else could I do
To stay alive? So at times I sniffed snow
Till I looked
Like a boneless bedspread.
Then I saw myself in the glass –
And stopped it at once.

Of course they tried to hang a dose
Of syphilis on me, but that
Was something they couldn't manage; they could only
      poison me
With arsenic: I had
Tubes in my side with
Pus flowing night and day. Who
Would have thought that a woman like me
Would ever make men crazy again? –
I began again at once.

I have never taken a man who did not do
Something for me, and had every man
I needed. By now I'm
Almost without feeling, almost gone dry
But
I'm beginning to fill up again, I have ups and downs, but
On the whole more ups.

I still notice myself calling my enemy
An old cow, and knowing her for my enemy because
A man looks at her.
But in a year
I'll have got over it –
I've already begun to.

I'm dirt; but everything
Must service my purpose, I'm
Coming up, I'm
Inevitable, the race of the future
Soon not dirt any more, but
The hard mortar with which
Cities are built.

(That's something I've heard a woman say.)

GIVE UP YOUR DREAMS

Give up your dream that they will make
An exception in your case.
What your mothers told you
Binds no one.

Keep your contracts in your pockets
They will not be honoured here.

Give up your hopes that you are all destined
To finish up Chairman.
Get on with your work.
You will need to pull yourselves together
If you are to be tolerated in the kitchen.

You still have to learn the ABC.
The ABC says:
They will get you down.

Do not think about what you have to say:
You will not be asked.
There are plenty of mouths for the meal
What's needed here is mincemeat.

(Not that anyone should be discouraged by that.)


FOUR INVITATIONS TO A MAN
AT DIFFERENT TIMES FROM
DIFFERENT QUARTERS

There's a home for you here
There's a room for your things.

Move the furniture about to suit yourself
Tell us what you need
Here is the key
Stay here.

There's a parlour for us all
And for you a room with a bed
You can work with us in the yard
You have your own plate
Stay with us.

Here's where you're to sleep
The sheets are still clean
They've only been slept in once.
If you're fussy
Rinse your tin spoon in the bucket there
It'll be as good as new
You're welcome to stay with us.

That's the room
Hurry up, or you can also stay
The night, but that costs extra.
I shan't disturb you
By the way, I'm not ill.
You'll be as well off here as anywhere else
So you might as well stay.


OFTEN AT NIGHT I DREAM

Often at night I dream I can
No longer earn my living.
Nobody in this country needs
The tables I make. The fishmongers speak
Chinese.

My closest relatives
Stare at me like a stranger
The woman I slept seven years with
Greets me politely on the landing and
Passes by
Smiling.

I know
That the last room already stands empty
The furniture has been cleared away
The mattress cut to ribbons
The curtains torn down.
In short everything has been got ready
To make my unhappy face
Go pale.

The linen hanging out to dry in the yard
Is my linen; I know it well.
Looking closer however I see
Darns in it and extra patches.
It seems
I have moved out. Someone else
Is living here now and
Doing so in
My linen.


SIT DOWN!

Sit down!
Are you seated?
You can lean right back.
You are to sit comfortably and at ease.
You may smoke.
It's important that you should hear me quite distinctly.
Can you hear me distinctly?
I have something to tell you which you will find of interest.

You are a flathead.
Can you really hear me?
I do hope there's no question of your not hearing me loud
        and clear?
Well:
I repeat: you are a flathead.
A flathead.
F as in Freddie, L as in Louis, A as in Annie, T as in Tommy
Head as in head.
Flathead.

Please do not interrupt me.
Don't interrupt me!
You are a flathead.
Don't say anything. No excuses!
You are a flathead.
Period.

I'm not the only one who says so.
Your respected mother has been saying it all along.
You are a flathead.
Just ask your relations
If you're not an F.
Of course no one tells you
Because you'd get vindictive, like any flathead.
But
Everyone round you has known for years you're an F.

It's characteristic that you should deny it.
That's just the point: it's characteristically F to deny it.
Oh, it's terribly hard to get a flathead to admit he's an F.
It's really exhausting.
Look, sooner or later it's got to be said
That you are an F.
It isn't entirely uninteresting to know what you are.
After all, it's a drawback not knowing what everyone
        knows.

Oh, you think you see things just like the other chap
But he's a flathead too.
Please don't comfort yourself that there are other Fs.
You are an F.

It's not too terrible
It won't stop you living to eighty.
In business it's a positive advantage.
And as for politics!
Invaluable!
As an F you have nothing to worry about
And you are an F.
(That's pleasant, isn't it?)

You still don't get it?
Well, who else do you want to tell you?
Brecht too says you're an F.
Come on, Brecht, give him your professional opinion.

The man's an F.
Well, then.

(This record needs to be played more than once.)


AGAIN AND AGAIN

Again and again
When I look at this man
He hasn't taken a drop and
He laughs as he used to
I think: it's getting better
Spring is coming, good times are coming
The times that are gone
Have returned
Love is beginning again, soon
Things will be like they once were.

Again and again
When I've been chatting with him
He has eaten his supper and doesn't go out
He is speaking to me and
Hasn't got his hat on
I think: it will be all right
Ordinary times are over
One can talk
To a chap, he listens
Love is beginning again, soon
Things will be just like they once were.

The rain
Never falls upwards.
When the wound
Stops hurting
What hurts is
The scar.

WHEN I SPEAK TO YOU

When I speak to you
Coldly and impersonally
Using the driest words
Without looking at you
(I seemingly fail to recognise you
In your particular nature and difficulty)

I speak to you merely
Like reality itself
(Sober, not to be bribed by your particular nature
Tired of your difficulty)
Which in my view you seem not to recognise.

ANNE SMITH RELATES THE CONQUEST OF AMERICA

In the beginning
It was grassland from the
Atlantic ocean to the still pacific sea
Bears and buffalo
Ran along the nameless Mississippi
And the red man
Ate their bloody flesh and his horse
The grass.
One day a man with white skin came
He roared and spewed out chunks of iron
When he was hungry and he was
Always hungry.
Red man murdered red man
Still on the river Mississippi but already
The white man passed by, some white men
With fiery water chunks of iron and the good book bible
And soon
There were chunks of iron in red men and bears and buffalo.
Three times one hundred years between the
Atlantic ocean and the silent pacific sea
The red man died
But
The rivers divided and the white man
Lifted the yellow metal out of them
And the ground tore apart under his hand
And out of it ran
The golden oil and all around
Wooden huts grew out of rotting grass and
Out of the wooden huts grew mountains of stone they were
Called cities. Into them went
The white people and said on the earth
A new age had broken out that is called: the Iron.
But the cities
Burned all night long
With the golden electricity

And by day
The decaying woods fell thundering upward: the trains.
Buffalo and red man
Had died out; however
There were oil and iron and gold more than water
And with music and shrieking the white people sat
In the eternal prairies of stone.
But the states that were there were called:
Arkansas, Connecticut, Ohio
New York, New Jersey and Massachusetts
And today still
There are oil and men and it is said
It is the greatest race on earth
That lives now and they all
Build houses and say
Mine is longer, and are there when there is oil
Ride in iron trains to the ends of the world
Grow wheat and sell it across the sea
And die no longer unknown but are
An eternal race in the earth's
Greatest age.


TERCETS ON LOVE

See those wild cranes in a great circle sweeping!
The clouds that lie behind them, soft and gentle
Started to drift with them as they were leaving
Their old life for a new one. Thus they went, all
At the same height and with the same haste soaring
Both of them seeming merely incidental.
That cloudbank and wild bird should thus fly sharing
The lovely sky which each so quickly covers
That therefore neither lingers in this clearing
And neither sees a thing except how wavers
The other in the wind which both feel brush them
Who now in flight lie alongside each other.

So into nothingness the wind may thrust them
If neither of them alters or disperses
So long will nothing have the power to touch them
So long can they be chased away from all these places
Where storms are threatening or shots re-echo.
So, under sun's and moon's but slightly differing faces
They fly away, each merging in his fellow.
Where going? . . . Nowhere much . . . Away from whom?
    . . . All of you.
That is a loving pair.
You may ask: how long have they been together? . . .
      A short while.
And how will they go on after? – Apart.
So lovers find in love a firm support.


JENNY'S SONG

1
Now, you gents, hear what my mother told me.
She thought me a shocking case:
I'd end on a slab in the mortuary
Or in some even more shocking place.
Well, that's the sort of thing a mother says.
Yes, but I'm telling you it doesn't count.
It won't put me off in the least.
If you want to know what comes of me, just wait!
A girl's not a beast.
   You lies in your bed as you made it
   For the law of the jungle is strict
   And it's me what is doing the kicking
   And it's you what is going to get kicked.

2
Now, you gents, hear what my fellow told me.
He gave me a look and said:
'Of all things on earth love's the greatest'

And 'Tomorrow's a long way ahead'.
Oh, 'love's' such an easy word to speak
But when you're growing older day by day
It's no longer love that you seek.
So best use the little time that's left you.
A girl's not a beast.
   You lies in your bed as you made it
   For the law of the jungle is strict
   And it's me what is doing the kicking
   And it's you what is going to get kicked.


PIRATE JENNY

Now you gents all see I've the glasses to wash.
When a bed's to be made I make it.
You may tip me with a penny, and I'll thank you very well
And you see me dressed in tatters, and this tatty old hotel
And you never ask how long I'll take it.
But one of these evenings there will be screams from the
      harbour
And they'll ask: what can all that screaming be?
And they'll see me smiling as I do the glasses
And they'll say: how she can smile beats me.
   And a ship with eight sails and
   All its fifty guns loaded
   Has tied up at the quay.

They say: get on, dry your glasses, my girl
And they tip me and don't give a damn.
And their penny is accepted, and their bed will be made
(Although nobody is going to sleep there, I'm afraid)
And they still have no idea who I am.
But one of these evenings there will be explosions from the
      harbour,
And they'll ask: what kind of a bang was that?
And they'll see me as I stand beside the window

And they'll say: what has she got to smile at?
  And that ship with eight sails and
  All its fifty guns loaded
  Will lay siege to the town.

Then you gents, you aren't going to find it a joke
For the walls will be knocked down flat
And in no time the town will be razed to the ground.
Just one tatty old hotel will be left standing safe and sound
And they'll ask: did someone special live in that?
Then there'll be a lot of people milling round the hotel
And they'll ask: what made them let that place alone?
And they'll see me as I leave the door next morning
And they'll say: don't tell us she's the one.
  And that ship with eight sails and
  All its fifty guns loaded
  Will run up its flag.

And a hundred men will land in the bright midday sun
Each stepping where the shadows fall.
They'll look inside each doorway and grab anyone they see
And put him in irons and then bring him to me
And they'll ask: which of these should we kill?
In that noonday heat there'll be a hush round the harbour
As they ask which has got to die.
And you'll hear me as I softly answer: the lot!
And as the first head rolls I'll say: hoppla!
  And that ship with eight sails and
  All its fifty guns loaded
  Will vanish with me.

THE SONG OF SURABAYA JOHNNY

I
I was just past my sixteenth birthday
When you drops in one day from the blue

And you says to come wiv' you to Burma
And to leave all the fixin' to you.
I asks you what job you was doing
And I swear that you answered to me
You was something to do with the railway
And 'ad nothing to do with the sea.
You talked a lot, Johnny
A lot of lies, Johnny
You took me for a ride, Johnny, all along the line.
I 'ates you so, Johnny
Your grinnin' there, Johnny –
Take that pipe out of your mouth, you swine.
    Surabaya Johnny, done the worst that you know.
    Surabaya Johnny, ah gawd, I love you so.
    Surabaya Johnny, where can I 'ide or go?
    You've got no 'eart, Johnny, yet I do love you so.

2

At first I was walkin' on roses
Till the day when I went off wiv' you
But I got on your nerves in a fortnight
And I guessed we was just about through.
We went 'iking all over the Punjab
Then driftin' downstream to the sea
Till I looks to meself in the mirror
Like a middle-aged 'ore on a spree.
You didn't want love, Johnny
You wanted cash, Johnny
I watched your mouth, Johnny, I knew the sign.
You asked a lot, Johnny
I gave you more, Johnny –
Take that pipe out of your mouth, you swine.
    Surabaya Johnny, done the worst that you know.
    Surabaya Johnny, ah gawd, I love you so.
    Surabaya Johnny, where can I 'ide or go?
    You've got no 'eart, Johnny, yet I do love you so.

3
I 'adn't the sense to wonder
'Ow you'd earned that particular name
But that coastline consisted of places
Where it turned out you often came.
One mornin' we'll wake in our lodgin's
And we'll hear the sea poundin' the rocks
And you'll get up and walk off in silence
'Cos your ship will be down at the docks.
You've got no 'eart, Johnny
You're no damn good, Johnny
You've gone away, Johnny, without a line.
I'm still in love, Johnny
Like at the start, Johnny –
Take that pipe out of your mouth, you swine.
   Surabaya Johnny, done the worst that you know.
   Surabaya Johnny, ah gawd, I love you so.
   Surabaya Johnny, where can I 'ide or go?
   You've got no 'eart, Johnny, yet I do love you so.


THE MANDALAY SONG

Mother Goddam's House in Mandalay
Dirty little hut beside the bay
Goddam, the finest knocking-shop you ever saw
With fifteen randy men in a queue outside the door
Watches in their hands, hip hip hooray!
Are they so short of tarts in Mandalay?
   Tarts are the best thing there is on earth
   And you always get your money's worth.
   Yes, in my opinion life would be ideal
   If the bloke before me weren't so bloody slow.
   Better fire your pistol through the keyhole –
   Make him realise he's holding up the show.
   Quicker, Johnny, hey! Quicker, Johnny, hey!
   While we sing the song of Mandalay:

Love is a sport to be kept within limits.
Johnny, be quick, for we're counting the minutes
And the moon won't shine forever on you, Mandalay.
And the moon won't shine forever on you.

Mother Goddam's House in Mandalay
Now it's at the bottom of the bay.
Goddam, the finest knocking-shop you ever saw
But where there was a queue once, there ain't a queue no
     more –
No more watches, no hip hip hooray.
All the tarts have gone from Mandalay.
  When you used to see tarts walk the earth
  Then you'd always get your money's worth.
  Now they've gone it's simply shattered our ideal.
  Knocking-shops like this one got dealt a mortal blow.
  Same goes for the gun and for the keyhole:
  Take away the tarts and you have wrecked the show.
  Quicker, Johnny, hey! Quicker, Johnny, hey!
  While we sing the song of Mandalay:
  Love is a sport to be kept within limits.
  Johnny, be quick, for we're counting the minutes
  And the moon won't shine forever on you, Mandalay.
  And the moon won't shine forever on you.

BALLAD OF SEXUAL OBSESSION

There goes an evil man who loves a battle:
The butcher, he. And all the others, cattle.
The cocky sod! No decent place lets him in.
Who does him down, that downs all others? Women.
Want it or not, he can't ignore that call.
Sexual obsession has him in its thrall.
  He doesn't read the Bible, sniggers at the law.
  Sets out to be an utter egotist
  And knows a woman's skirts are what he must resist

So when a woman calls he locks his door.
So far, so good, but what's the future brewing?
As soon as night falls he'll be up and doing.

Thus many a man observed the sad conclusion:
A mighty genius, stuck on prostitution!
While as for those whose urges were exhausted
Once they'd collapsed, who paid the funeral? Whores did.
Want it or not, they can't ignore that call.
Sexual obsession has them in its thrall.
   Some fall back on the Bible. Some set out to change the
      law.
   Some turn to Christ, and some turn anarchist.
   At lunch you pick the best wine on the list
   And then you meditate on what life's for.
   At tea: what noble aims you are pursuing!
   Then soon as night falls you are up and doing.

There stands a man. The gallows loom above him.
They've got the quicklime mixed in which to shove him.
They've put his neck just under where the noose is
And what's he thinking of, the idiot? Floozies.
They've all but hanged him, yet he hears the call.
Sexual obsession has him in its thrall.
   She's sold him down the river, shopped him heart and
      soul
   He's seen the filthy money in her hand.
   And bit by bit begins to understand:
   The pit that covers him is woman's hole.
   Then he may rant and roar and curse his ruin –
   But soon as night falls he'll be up and doing.

## BALLAD OF IMMORAL EARNINGS

There was a time, now very far away
When we set up together, I and she.
I'd got the brains, and she supplied the breast.
I saw her right, and she looked after me –
A way of life then, if not quite the best.
And when a client came I'd slide out of our bed
And treat him nice, and go and have a drink instead
And when he paid up I'd address him: Sir
Come any time you feel you fancy her.
Those days are past, but what would I now give
To see that whorehouse where we used to live?

That was the time, now very far away
He was so sweet and bashed me where it hurt.
And when the cash ran out the feathers really flew
He'd up and say: I'm going to pawn your skirt.
A skirt is nicer, but no skirt will do.
Just like his cheek, he had me fairly stewing
I'd ask him what the hell he fancied he was doing
Then he'd lash out and knock me down the stairs.
I had the bruises off and on for years.
Those days are past, but what would I now give
To see that whorehouse where we used to live?

That was the time, now very far away –
Not that the bloody times seem to have looked up
When afternoons were all I had for you
(I told you she was generally booked up.
The night's more normal, but daytime will do).
Once I was pregnant, so the doctor said.
So we reversed positions on the bed.
He thought his weight might make it premature.
But in the end we flushed it down the sewer.
That could not last, but what would I now give
To see that whorehouse where we used to live?

THE CANNON SONG

John was all present and Jim was all there
And Georgie was up for promotion.
Not that the army gave a bugger who they were
When confronting some heathen commotion.
   The troops live under
   The cannon's thunder
   From the Cape to Cooch Behar.
   Moving from place to place
   When they come face to face
   With a different breed of fellow
   Whose skin is black or yellow
   They quick as winking chop him into beefsteak tartare.

Johnny found his whisky too warm
And Jim found the weather too balmy
But Georgie took them both by the arm
And said: never let down the army.
   The troops live under
   The cannon's thunder
   From the Cape to Cooch Behar.
   Moving from place to place
   When they come face to face
   With a different breed of fellow
   Whose skin is black or yellow
   They quick as winking chop him into beefsteak tartare.

John is a write-off and Jimmy is dead
And they shot poor old Georgie for looting
But young men's blood goes on being red
And the army goes on recruiting.
   The troops live under
   The cannon's thunder
   From the Cape to Cooch Behar.
   Moving from place to place
   When they come face to face

With a different breed of fellow
Whose skin is black or yellow
They quick as winking chop him into beefsteak tartare.


## BALLAD OF MAC THE KNIFE

See the shark with teeth like razors.
All can read his open face.
And Macheath has got a knife, but
Not in such an obvious place.

See the shark, how red his fins are
As he slashes at his prey.
Mac the Knife wears white kid gloves which
Give the minimum away.

By the Thames's turbid waters
Men abruptly tumble down.
Is it plague or is it cholera?
Or a sign Macheath's in town?

On a beautiful blue Sunday
See a corpse stretched in the Strand.
See a man dodge round the corner . . .
Mackie's friends will understand.

And Schmul Meier, reported missing
Like so many wealthy men:
Mac the Knife acquired his cash box.
God alone knows how or when.

Jenny Towler turned up lately
With a knife stuck through her breast
While Macheath walks the Embankment
Nonchalantly unimpressed.

Where is Alfred Gleet the cabman?
Who can get that story clear?
All the world may know the answer
Just Macheath has no idea.

And the ghastly fire in Soho –
Seven children at a go –
In the crowd stands Mac the Knife, but he
Isn't asked and doesn't know.

And the child-bride in her nightie
Whose assailant's still at large
Violated in her slumbers –
Mackie, how much did you charge?


SECOND THREEPENNY FINALE
WHAT KEEPS MANKIND ALIVE?

You gentlemen who think you have a mission
To purge us of the seven deadly sins
Should first sort out the basic food position
Then start your preaching: that's where it begins.
You lot, who preach restraint and watch your waist as
       well
Should learn for all time how the world is run:
However much you twist, whatever lies you tell
Food is the first thing. Morals follow on.
So first make sure that those who now are starving
Get proper helpings when we do the carving.
    What keeps mankind alive? The fact that millions
    Are daily tortured, stifled, punished, silenced,
         oppressed.
    Mankind can keep alive thanks to its brilliance
    In keeping its humanity repressed.
    For once you must try not to shirk the facts:
    Mankind is kept alive by bestial acts.

You say that girls may strip with your permission.
You draw the line dividing art from sin.
So first sort out the basic food position
Then start your preaching: that's where we begin.
You lot, who bank on your desires and our disgust
Should learn for all time how the world is run:
Whatever lies you tell, however much you twist
Food is the first thing. Morals follow on.
So first make sure that those who now are starving
Get proper helpings when we do the carving.
   What keeps mankind alive? The fact that millions
   Are daily tortured, stifled, punished, silenced,
      oppressed.
   Mankind can keep alive thanks to its brilliance
   In keeping its humanity repressed.
   For once you must try not to shirk the facts:
   Mankind is kept alive by bestial acts.


## THE UNEMPLOYED

You who have just
Come from your food
Permit us to tell you of our
Unceasing concern with food like yours
(Not that something more modest would not do).

We ask you: observe us
In our unceasing search for work.
Too bad that food and work
Are subject to immutable laws
Unknown ones.

Yet ever are falling
Downwards
Through gratings in the metalled streets
All kinds of people without marks

Or description to identify them, downwards
Suddenly, silently, quickly downwards
Snatched out of the mainstream of humanity according to
No clear principle
Six out of seven downwards, but the seventh
Enters the food room.

Which of us is it? Who
Has been detailed to be saved?
Who is marked out?
Where is the grating that's nearest?
– Unknown.

## ONCE AGAIN MAN'S HANDIWORK CRUMBLES

Once again man's handiwork crumbles.
That which cost so much effort.
That which caused so many tears
And for which so much blood was shed, those works
Are foundering.

The dwellings crumble. In them henceforward will live
Fungus. Into the machine-rooms
Moves the crack-up. Across the railway tracks
Goes the evening wind, for none but the wind still visits
The tottering derricks and once
Powerful cranes, now given over
To their last proprietor, the
All-consuming rust.

The goatherd
Takes his surviving goats round the barbed wire.
The peasant
Again tugs his spade from the soil, a peasant once more
But a peasant without land, no longer a peasant.
For the field that once grew hay
Has become a scrapheap and now grows nothing.

Once again the rock raises its mighty shoulder
The grass moves in again. The thickets tangle.
And yet
Were oil to be required in the cities and between cities
It would be lying where the grass grows.

You, though, who saw the battles that were fought
Ingenuity of men's brains, force that strikes
Saw great efforts on all sides, now you know
How much effort it cost not
To produce oil.

## SONG OF THE STIMULATING IMPACT OF CASH

### 1

People keep on saying cash is sordid
Yet this world's a cold place if you're short.
Not so once you can afford it
And have ample cash support.
No need then to feel you've been defrauded
Everything is bathed in rosy light
Warming all you set your eyes on
Giving each what's his by right.
Sunshine spreads to the horizon.
Just watch the smoke; the fire's alight.
    Then things soon become as different as they can.
    Longer views are taken. Hearts beat harder.
    Proper food to eat. Looking much smarter.
    And your man is quite a different man.

### 2

O you're all so hopelessly mistaken
If you think cash flow has no effect.
Fertile farms produce no bacon
When the water-pump's been wrecked.
Now men grab as much as they can collect.

Once they'd standards they used not to flout.
If your belly's full you don't start shooting.
Now there's so much violence about.
Father, mother, brothers put the boot in.
Look, no more smoke now: the fire's gone out.
   Everything explodes, incendiaries are hurled
   Smash-and-grab's the rule; it's a disaster.
   Every little servant thinks he's master
   And the world's a very bitter world.

3
That's the fate of all that's noble and splendid
People quickly write it off as trash
Since with empty stomach and unmended
Footwear nobody's equipped to cut a dash.
They don't want what's good, they want the cash
And their instinct's to be mean and tight.
But when Right has got the cash to back it
It's got what it takes to see it right.
Never mind your dirty little racket
Just watch the smoke now: the fire's alight.
   Then you start believing in humanity once more:
   Everyone's a saint, as white as plaster.
   Principles grow stronger. Just like before.
   Wider views are taken. Hearts beat faster.
   You can tell the servant from the master.
   So the law is once again the law.

BALLAD OF GOOD LIVING

I've heard them praising single-minded spirits
Whose empty stomachs show they live for knowledge
In the rat-infested shacks awash with ullage.
I'm all for culture, but there are some limits.
The simple life is fine for those it suits.
I don't find, for my part, that it attracts.

There's not a bird from here to Halifax
Would peck at such unappetising fruits.
What use is freedom? None, to judge from this.
One must live well to know what living is.

The dashing sort who cut precarious capers
And go and risk their necks just for the pleasure
Then swagger home and write it up at leisure
And flog the story to the Sunday papers –
If you could see how cold they get at night
Sullen, with chilly wife, climbing to bed
And how they dream they're going to get ahead
And see the future stretching out of sight –
Now tell me, who would choose to live like this?
One must live well to know what living is.

There's plenty that they have. I know I lack it
And ought to join their splendid isolation
But when I gave it more consideration
I told myself: my friend, that's not your racket.
Suffering ennobles, but it can depress.
The paths of glory lead but to the grave.
You once were poor and lonely, wise and brave.
You ought to try to bite off rather less.
The search for happiness boils down to this:
One must live well to know what living is.


NEW ENDING TO THE
BALLAD OF MAC THE KNIFE
(*film version*)

So we reach our happy ending.
Rich and poor can now embrace.
Once the cash is not a problem
Happy endings do take place.

Don't you fish in troubled waters
Said the heiress to the whore.
Now they share luxurious quarters
Sponging on the starving poor.

Some in light and some in darkness.
That's the kind of world we mean.
Those you see are in the light part.
Those in darkness don't get seen.


## SONG OF THE SA MAN

My hunger made me fall asleep
With a belly ache.
Then I heard voices crying
Hey, Germany awake!

Then I saw crowds of men marching:
To the Third Reich, I heard them say.
I thought, as I'd nothing left to live for
I might as well march their way.

The chief of staff wore boots
My feet meanwhile got wet
But both of us were marching
Wholeheartedly in step.

I thought that the left road led forward.
He told me that I was wrong.
I went the way that he ordered
And blindly tagged along.

They told me which enemy to shoot at.
I accepted their gun and aimed
And, when I had shot, saw my brother
Was the enemy they had named.

So now my brother is dying
By my own hand he fell.
Yet I know that if he's defeated
I shall be lost as well.


## ALTER THE WORLD, IT NEEDS IT

Whom would the just man fail to greet, in order to stop an
    injustice?
What medicine tastes too nasty to save
A dying man?
How much meanness would you not commit if the aim is
To stamp out meanness?
If you'd found a way to alter this planet, what would you
Refuse to do?
What would you refuse to do?
Sink deep in the mire
Shake hands with the butcher: yes, but
Alter the world, it needs it!
Who are you?


## PRAISE OF THE PARTY

Who do you think is the Party?
Does it sit in a big house with a switchboard?
Are all its decisions unknown, all its thoughts wrapped in
    secrecy?
Who is it?
We are it.
You and I and them – all of us.
Comrade, the clothes it's dressed in are your clothes, the
    head that it thinks with is yours
Where I'm lodging, there is its house, and where you suffer
    an assault it fights back.

Show us the path we must take, and we
Shall take it with you, but
Don't take the right path without us.
Without us it is
The most wrong of all.
Don't cut yourself off from us!
We can go astray and you can be right, so
Don't cut yourself off from us!

That the short path is better than the long one can't be
    denied.
But if someone knows it
And cannot point it out to us, what use is his wisdom?
Be wise with us.
Don't cut yourself off from us!

One single man may have two eyes
But the Party has a thousand.
One single man may see a town
But the Party sees six countries.
One single man can spare a moment
The Party has many moments.
One single man can be obliterated
But the Party can't be obliterated
For its methods are those of its philosophers
Which are based on experience of reality
And are destined soon to transform it
As soon as the masses make them their own.


THE SPRING

The play of the sexes renews itself
In the springtime. That's when the young lovers come
    together.
Just one gentle caress from the hand of her loved one
Makes the young girl's breast start to tremble.
Her merest glance can overwhelm him.

A new-found light
Reveals the countryside to lovers in springtime.
The air's turning warm.
The days start getting long and the
Fields stay light a long while.

Boundless is the growth of all trees and all grasses
In springtime.
And incessantly fruitful
Is the land, are the meadows, the forest.
And then the earth gives birth to the new
Heedless of caution.

## SOLELY BECAUSE OF THE INCREASING DISORDER

Solely because of the increasing disorder
In our cities of class struggle
Some of us have now decided
To speak no more of cities by the sea, snow on roofs,
          women
The smell of ripe apples in cellars, the senses of the flesh, all
That makes a man round and human
But to speak in future only about the disorder
And so become one-sided, reduced, enmeshed in the
          business
Of politics and the dry, indecorous vocabulary
Of dialectical economics
So that this awful cramped coexistence
Of snowfalls (they're not merely cold, we know)
Exploitation, the lured flesh, class justice, should not
          engender
Approval of a world so many-sided; delight in
The contradictions of so bloodstained a life.
You understand.

REPORT FROM GERMANY

We learn that in Germany
In the days of the brown plague
On the roof of an engineering works suddenly
A red flag fluttered in the November wind
The outlawed flag of freedom!
In the grey mid-November from the sky
Fell rain mixed with snow
It was the 7th, though: day of the Revolution!

And look! the red flag!

The workers stand in the yards
Shield their eyes with their hands and stare
At the roof through the flurries of icy rain.

Then lorries roll up filled with stormtroopers
And they drive to the wall any who wear work clothes
And with cords bind any fists that are calloused
And from the sheds after their interrogation
Stumble the beaten and bloody
Not one of whom has named the man
Who was on the roof.

So they drive away those who kept silent
And the rest have had enough.
But next day there waves again
The red flag of the proletariat
On the engineering works roof. Again
Thuds through the dead-still town
The stormtroopers' tread. In the yards
There are no men to be seen now. Only women
Stand with stony faces; hands shielding their eyes, they gaze
At the roof through the flurries of icy rain.

And the beatings begin once more. Under interrogation
The women testify: that flag
Is a bedsheet in which
We bore away one who died yesterday.
You can't blame us for the colour it is.
It is red with the murdered man's blood, you should know.


## BALLAD OF MARIE SANDERS, THE 'JEWS' WHORE'

### 1

In Nuremberg they enacted a law
At which many a woman wept who'd
Not been sleeping with the proper breed of man.
    'The price is rising for butcher's meat.
    The drumming's now at its height.
    God alive, if they are coming down our street
    It'll be tonight.'

### 2

Marie Sanders, your young lover's got too black a head.
Take our advice, and don't you be to him
What you were yesterday.
    'The price is rising for butcher's meat.
    The drumming's now at its height.
    God alive, if they are coming down our street
    It'll be tonight.'

### 3

Mother, give me the latchkey
It can't really be so bad
The moon looks just as bright as ever.
    'The price is rising for butcher's meat.
    The drumming's now at its height.
    God alive, if they are coming down our street
    It'll be tonight.'

4

But one morning, close on nine
She was driven through the town
Round her neck a sign, her hair all shaven.
The street was yelling. She
Stared ahead.
   'The price is rising for butcher's meat.
   And Streicher is speaking tonight.
   God alive, if they understood his speech
   They would start to make sense of their plight.'

## BUT FOR THE JEWS ADVISING AGAINST IT

But for the Jews advising against it
The King of England would offer our Chancellor his Indian
     empire, saying
Just help yourself. And the French Assembly has
Long harboured the desire to bestow the mineral resources
    of Lorraine
On our Chancellor, whose
Moustache it so admires. Only
The Jews would not allow it.

Until the Führer told us, we had no idea
What a clever and powerful people the Jews were.
Though there are only a few of them scattered across the
    earth's face
It seems that they control everything because of their
    genius.
At the sound of their softest whistle
The British lion rolls on its back and wags its tail.
Mighty New York, towering up into the heavens, fears
    Jewry's frown more than any earthquake.
And the Pope eats out of its hand.
This being so, the entire world asks itself with a shudder
What would happen to the global structure

If the Führer had chosen for his lofty purposes
Not the relatively talented Germans, but
The Jews.

## LETTER TO THE NEW YORK WORKERS' COMPANY 'THEATRE UNION' ABOUT THE PLAY *THE MOTHER*

1
When I wrote the play *The Mother*
On the basis of the book by comrade Gorky and of many
Proletarian comrades' stories about their
Daily struggle, I wrote it
With no frills, in austere language
Placing the words cleanly, carefully selecting
My character's every gesture, as is done
When reporting the words and deeds of the great.
I did my best to
Portray those seemingly ordinary
Countless incidents in contemptible dwellings
Among the far too many-headed as historical incidents
In no way less significant than the renowned
Acts of generals and statesmen in the school books.
The task I gave myself was to tell of a great historic figure
The unknown early champion of humanity
To constitute an example.

2
So you will see the proletarian mother take the road
The long and winding road of her class, see how at the start
She feels the loss of a penny on her son's wages: she cannot
Make him a soup worth eating. So she engages
In a struggle with him, fears she may lose him. Then
Reluctantly she aids him in his struggle for that penny
Ever fearful now of losing him to the struggle. Slowly
She follows her son into the jungle of wage claims. Thereby
She learns to read. Quits her hut, cares for others

Beside her son, in the same situation as he, those with
    whom she
Earlier struggled over her son; now she struggles alongside
    them.
Thus the walls around her stove start to tumble. Her table
    welcomes
Many another mother's son. Once too small for two
Her hut becomes a meeting place. Her son, though
She seldom sees. The struggle takes him from her.
And she herself is among the throng of those struggling.
    The talk
Between son and mother grows into a rallying-cry
During the battle. In the end the son falls. No longer was it
Possible for her to provide him with his soup by the one
Available means. But now she is standing
In the thichest turmoil of the vast and
Unceasing battle of the classes. Still a mother
Now even more a mother, mother of many now fallen
Mother of fighters, mother of unborn generations, she
    embarks
On a spring-clean of the State. Gives the rulers stones
In their extorted feast. Cleans weapons. Teaches
Her sons and daughters the ABC of struggle
Against war and exploitation, member of a standing army
Covering the entire planet, harried and harrying
Untolerated and intolerant. Defeated and relentless.


3
So too we staged the play like a report from a great epoch
No less golden in the light of many lamps than the
Royal plays staged in earlier times
No less cheerful and funny, discreet
In its sad moments. Before a clean canvas
The players entered simply with the characteristic
Gests of their scenes, delivering their phrases
Precisely, authentic words. Each phrase's effect
Was awaited and exposed. And also we waited

Till the crowd had laid those phrases in the balance – for we
    had noticed
How the man who owns little and is often deceived will bite
A coin with his teeth to see if it is genuine. Just like coins
    then
Must the actors' phrases be tested by our spectators
Who own little and are often deceived. Small hints
Suggested the scene of the action. The odd table and chair:
Bare essentials were enough. But photographs
Of the great opponents were projected on the screens at the
    back
And the sayings of the socialist classics
Painted on banners or projected on screens, surrounded the
Scrupulous actors. Their bearing was natural
Yet whatever said nothing was left out in the
Carefully considered abridgement. The musical numbers
Were lightly presented, with charm. Much laughter
Filled the house. The unconquerable
Good humour of the resourceful Vlassova, grounded in the
    assurance of
Her youthful class, provoked
Happy laughs from the workers' benches.
Keenly they took advantage of this rare chance
To experience the usual incidents without urgent danger,
    thus
Getting the leisure to study them and so prepare
Their own conduct.

4
Comrades, I see you
Reading the short play with embarrassment.
The spare language
Seems like poverty. This report, you reckon
Is not how people express themselves. I have read
Your adaptation. Here you insert a 'Good morning'
There a 'Hullo, my boy'. The vast field of action
Gets cluttered with furniture. Cabbage reeks

From the stove. What's bold becomes gallant, what's
　　historical normal.
Instead of wonder
You strive for sympathy with the mother when she loses her
　　son.
The son's death
You slyly put at the end. That, you think, is how to make
　　the spectator
Keep up his interest till the curtain falls. Like a business man
Investing money in a concern, you suppose, the spectator
　　invests
Feeling in the hero: he wants to get it back
If possible doubled. But the proletarian audience
At the first performance never missed the son at the end.
They maintained their interest. Not out of crudeness either.
And then too we were sometimes asked:
Will the workers understand you? Will they renounce
The familiar opiate: the spiritual participation
In other people's anger, in the rise of others, the whole
　　deception
That whips one up for two hours, to leave one still more
　　exhausted
Filled with hazy memories and yet vaguer expectations?
Will you truly, offering
Knowledge and experience, get an audience of statesmen?

Comrades, the form of the new plays
Is new, but why be
Frightened of what's new? Is it hard to bring off?
But why be frightened of what's new and hard to bring off?
To the man who's exploited, continually deceived
Life itself is a perpetual experiment
The earning of a few pennies
An uncertain business which is nowhere taught.
Why should he fear the new rather than the old? And even if
Your audience, the workers, hesitated you should still
Not lag behind it but show it the way

Swiftly show it the way with long strides, its final power
    inspiring you
With unbounded confidence.


THE PLAYWRIGHT'S SONG

I am a playwright. I show
What I have seen. In the man markets
I have seen how men are traded. That
I show, I, the playwright.

How they step into each other's rooms with schemes
Or rubber truncheons, or with cash
How they stand in the streets and wait
How they lay traps for one another
Full of hope
How they make appointments
How they hang each other
How they make love
How they defend their loot
How they eat
I show all that.

The words which they call out to each other I report.
What the mother says to her son
What the employer tells the employee
What the wife replies to her husband
All the begging words, all the commanding
The grovelling, the misleading
The lying, the unknowing
The winning, the wounding . . .
I report them all.

I see snowstorms making their entrances
I see earthquakes coming forward
I see mountains blocking the road

And rivers I see breaking their banks.
But the snowstorms have hats on
The earthquakes have money in their wallet
The mountains came in a conveyance
And the headlong rivers control the police.
That I reveal.

To learn how to show what I see
I read up the representations of other peoples and other
        periods.
One or two plays I have adapted, precisely
Checking the technique of those times and absorbing
Whatever is of use to me.
I studied the portrayal of the great feudal figures
By the English, of rich individuals
To whom the world existed for their fuller development.
I studied the moralising Spaniards
The Indians, masters of beautiful sensations
And the Chinese, who portray the family
And the many-coloured destinies found in cities.

And so swiftly did the appearance of cities and houses
Change in my time that to go away for two years
And come back was like a trip to another city
And people in vast numbers changed their appearance
Within a few years. I saw
Workers enter the factory gates, and the gateway was tall
But when they came out they had to bend.
Then I told myself:
Everything alters and is for its own time only.

And so I gave each setting its recognition mark
And branded the figures of the year on each factory yard
        and each room
Like drovers who brand figures on their cattle to identify
        them.
And the sentences too that were spoken there

I gave recognition marks to, so that they became like the
    sayings
Of impermanent men which are set down
So that they may not be forgotten.

What the woman in overalls said during those years
Bent over her leaflets
And the way the brokers used yesterday to speak to their
    clerks
Hats on the backs of their heads
I marked with the impermanence of
Their year of origin.

But all this I yielded up to astonishment
Even the most familiar part of it.
That a mother gave her child the breast
I reported like something no one would believe.
That a porter slammed the door in a freezing man's face
Like something nobody had ever seen.


THE MOMENT BEFORE IMPACT

I speak my lines before
The audience hears them; what they will hear is
Something done with. Every word that leaves the lip
Describes an arc, and then
Falls on the listener's ear; I wait and hear
The way it strikes; I know
We are not feeling the same thing and
We are not feeling it at the same time.

## LETTER TO THE PLAYWRIGHT ODETS

Comrade, in your play *Paradise Lost* you show
That the families of the exploiters
Are destroyed in the end.
What do you mean by that?

It could be that the families of the exploiters
Are destroyed. But what if they're not?
Do they cease to exploit when they go to pieces or
Is it easier for us to be exploited so long
As they've not gone to pieces? Should the hungry man
Continue to be hungry, so long as he who refuses him bread
Is a healthy man?

Or do you mean to tell us that our exploiters
Have already been weakened? Should we
Just sit there, waiting? Such pictures
Our house painter painted, comrade, and overnight
We felt the strength of our exploiters who'd gone to pieces.

Or should you feel sorry for them? Should we
Burst into tears when we see the bedbugs move out?
You, comrade, who showed compassion towards the man
Who has nothing to eat, do you now feel compassion
For the man who has stuffed himself sick?

## THE ACTRESS IN EXILE
(dedicated to Helen Weigel)

Now she makes up. In the white cubicle
She sits forward, on the edge of the makeshift stool
Putting on her greasepaint before the mirror
With easy gestures.
Carefully she rids her face of
Everything remarkable: it will reflect

The quietest reaction. Now and then
She lets her fine supple shoulders
Fall forward, as do those who
Work hard. Already she wears the coarse blouse
With a patch on the sleeve. The rope slippers are still
Standing on the table.
Once ready, she
Wants to know if the drum has arrived
On which the cannonade is sounded, and whether the big
      net
Has been hung. Then she stands up, a small figure, a
Great battler
To step into the rope slippers and portray
The battle of an Andalusian fisherwoman
Against the generals.


## AN ACTRESS SOLILOQUISES WHILE MAKING UP

I am portraying a drinker
Who sells her children
In Paris at the time of the Commune.
I only have five lines.

But I also have to walk up the street.
I shall walk like someone who has been liberated
Whom nobody ever wanted to
Liberate except from gin, and I shall
Look around me as drunks do, who are afraid
Of being followed, look around me
At the audience.

I have checked my five lines like documents
Which one washes with acid for signs of any writing
Beneath what appears there. I shall
Speak each one of them like an indictment
Of myself and all who are watching me.

If I did not think, I would make up
Like an old soak
Somebody ill or down and out, but I shall come on
As someone beautiful but wrecked
By a yellow, once-white complexion, now ravaged but
Once attractive, now a scarecrow
So that everyone asks: Who
Did that?

EMIGRANT'S LAMENT

I earned my bread and ate it just like you.
I am a doctor; or at least I was.
The colour of my hair, shape of my nose
Cost me my home, my bread and butter too.

She who for seven years had slept with me
My hand upon her lap, her face against my face
Took me to court. The cause of my disgrace:
My hair was black. So she got rid of me.

But I escaped at night-time through a wood
(Endangered by my mother's ancestry)
To find a country that would be my host.

Yet when I asked for work it was no good.
You are impertinent, they said to me.
I'm not impertinent, I said: I'm lost.

SONNET NO. 19

My one requirement: that you stay with me.
I want to hear you, grumble as you may.
If you were deaf I'd need what you might say
If you were dumb I'd need what you might see.

If you were blind I'd want you in my sight
For you're the sentry posted to my side:
We're hardly half way through our lengthy ride
Remember we're surrounded yet by night.

Your 'let me lick my wounds' is no excuse now.
Your 'anywhere' (not here) is no defence
There'll be relief for you, but no release now.

You know whoever's needed can't go free
And you are needed urgently by me
I speak of me when us would make more sense.

SONNET NO. 1

And now it's war; our path is growing steeper.
You, my companion sent to share the journey
On broad or narrow roads, on smooth or stony
A student each of us, and each a teacher

And each now fleeing for the selfsame end
Know what I know: This end cannot be counted
More than the journey, so that if one fainted
And if the other left him, all intent

To gain his end, why, it would surely vanish
Not to be seen again, or found by asking.
Breathless he'd run until he stood in panic

Sweating, in grey and neutral nothingness.
To tell you this, and mark the point we're passing
I put my message in poetic dress.


FINNISH LANDSCAPE

Those fish-stocked waters! Such splendid trees as well!
Scent of the berries and the birches there!
Concord of winds that gently lull an air
So milky that those clanking iron churns
That trundle from the white farmhouse might be open!
Bemused by sight and sound and sense and smell
The refugee beneath the alders turns
Once more to his laborious task: of hoping.

He counts the corn stooks, sees which cows have strayed
Down to the lake, hears moos from their strong lungs
But also knows who's short of milk and corn.
Faced with the barge that takes logs to be sawn
He asks: Is that how wooden legs are made?
And meets a people silent in two tongues.


IN FAVOUR OF A LONG, BROAD SKIRT

Your ample peasant skirt's the one to pick
Where cunningly I emphasise the length:
Lifting it off you to its full extent
Revealing thighs and bottom, gives a kick.

Then when you tuck your legs up on our sofa
Let it ride up, so that, hidden in its shadow
Through deep discussions clouded in tobacco
Your flesh may hint our night is not yet over.

It is more than a base and lustful feeling
That makes me want a skirt as wide as this:
Your lovely movements bring to mind Colchis
The day Medea strolled towards the sea. –
These aren't the grounds, though, on which I'm appealing
For such a skirt. Base ones will do for me.


PARADE OF THE OLD NEW

I stood on a hill and I saw the Old approaching, but it came
as the New.

It hobbled up on new crutches which no one had ever
seen before and stank of new smells of decay which no one
had ever smelt before.

The stone that rolled past was the newest invention and
the screams of the gorillas drumming on their chests set up
to be the newest musical composition.

Everywhere you could see open graves standing empty as
the New advanced on the capital.

Round about stood such as inspired terror, shouting:
Here comes the New, it's all new, salute the New, be new
like us! And those who heard, heard nothing but their
shouts, but those who saw, saw such as were not shouting.

So the Old strode in disguised as the New, but it brought
the New with it in its triumphal procession and presented it
as the Old.

The New went fettered and in rags; they revealed its
splendid limbs.

And the procession moved through the night, but what
they thought was the light of dawn was the light of fires in

the sky. And the cry: Here comes the New, it's all new, salute the New, be new like us! would have been easier to hear if all had not been drowned in a thunder of guns.

## GREAT BABEL GIVES BIRTH

When her time was come she withdrew into her innermost chamber and surrounded herself with doctors and sooth-sayers.

There was whispering. Solemn men went into the house with grave faces and came out with anxious faces that were pale. And the price of white make-up doubled in the beauty shops.

In the street the people gathered and stood from morning till night with empty stomachs.

The first sound that was heard was like a mighty fart in the rafters, followed by a mighty cry of PEACE!, whereupon the stink became greater.

Immediately after that, blood spurted up in a thin watery jet. And now came further sounds in unceasing succession, each more terrible than the last.

Great Babel vomited and it sounded like FREEDOM! and coughed and it sounded like JUSTICE! and farted again and it sounded like PROSPERITY! And wrapped in a bloody sheet a squalling brat was carried on to the balcony and shown to the people with ringing of bells, and it was WAR.

And it had a thousand fathers.

## ROLL-CALL OF THE VIRTUES AND THE VICES

An Oppression Evening was held recently at which, to a fanfare of trombones, a number of prominent personalities appeared as a demonstration of their solidarity with those in power.

*Vindictiveness*, with a get-up and hairstyle like those

worn by Conscience, displayed her infallible memory. Small and crippled, she was greeted with thunderous applause.

An unfortunate entrance was made by *Brutality*. Looking distractedly around her, she lost her footing on the dais, but made up for this by angrily stamping on the floor hard enough to make a hole in it.

She was followed by *Resentment*, who with frothing lips appealed to the ignorant to cast off the burdens of knowledge. 'Down with the know-alls!' was his cry; after which the know-nothings bore him from the hall on their worn shoulders.

*Smarminess* too put in an appearance and proved herself a mighty scrounger. On her way out she bowed to one or two fat swindlers whom she had helped to high positions.

An old favourite, the soubrette *Schadenfreude*, provided one of the brighter spots. Unhappily she suffered a minor accident by laughing till her ribs bust.

First to appear in Part Two of this competitive show was that well-known sportsman *Ambition*. He jumped so high in the air that he hurt his tiny head against one of the rafters. Both then and later, when a steward pinned a medal with a long pin straight into his flesh, his upper lip remained stiff.

Looking a little pale, possibly from stage fright, *Justice* introduced herself. She spoke of trivialities and promised to give a comprehensive lecture any day now.

That strapping young fellow *Curiosity* talked about how the regime had opened his eyes, likewise about the responsibility of hooked noses for bad public administration.

An appearance was put in by *Self-Sacrifice*, a tall stringy individual with an honest face and a large imitation pewter plate in his calloused hand. He was collecting pennies off the workers and repeating softly in a weary voice 'Remember the children'.

*Order* too came on the dais, her spotless cap covering her hairless head. She awarded medical diplomas to the liars and surgical degrees to the murderers. Despite having been out all night thieving from backyard dustbins, she had not a speck of dust on her grey dress. A long and apparently endless queue of the robbed filed past her table as with arthritic hands she wrote each of them a receipt. Her sister *Economy* displayed a basket full of crusts which she had torn from the lips of patients in the hospitals.

With weals on his neck, and gasping for air as if being driven to death, *Hard Work* gave a free demonstration. In less time than it takes to blow your nose he machined a shell-case, while as an encore he brewed poison gas enough for two thousand families before you could say Jack Robinson.

All these famous persons, the children and grandchildren of *Cold* and *Hunger*, appeared before the people and unreservedly proclaimed themselves the servants of *Oppression*.

## THE BUDDHA'S PARABLE OF THE BURNING HOUSE

Gautama the Buddha taught
The doctrine of greed's wheel to which we are bound, and
      advised
That we should shed all craving and thus
Undesiring enter the nothingness that he called Nirvana.
Then one day his pupils asked him:
What is it like, this nothingness, Master? Every one of us
      would
Shed all craving, as you advise, but tell us
Whether this nothingness which then we shall enter
Is perhaps like being at one with all creation
When you lie in water, your body weightless, at noon
Unthinking almost, lazily lie in the water, or drowse
Hardly knowing now that you straighten the blanket
Going down fast – whether this nothingness, then
Is a happy one of this kind, a pleasant nothingness, or
Whether this nothing of yours is mere nothing, cold,
      senseless and void.
Long the Buddha was silent, then said nonchalantly:
There is no answer to your question.
But in the evening, when they had gone
The Buddha still sat under the bread-fruit tree, and to the
      others
To those who had not asked, addressed this parable:
Lately I saw a house. It was burning. The flame
Licked at its roof. I went up close and observed
That there were people still inside. I opened the door and
      called
Out to them that the roof was ablaze, so exhorting them
To leave at once. But those people
Seemed in no hurry. One of them
When the heat was already scorching his eyebrows
Asked me what it was like outside, whether it wasn't raining
Whether the wind wasn't blowing perhaps, whether there
      was

Another house for them, and more of this kind. Without
    answering
I went out again. These people here, I thought
Need to burn to death before they stop asking questions.
    Truly, friends
Unless a man feels the ground so hot underfoot that he'd
    gladly
Exchange it for any other, sooner than stay, to him
I have nothing to say. Thus Gautama the Buddha.
But we too, no longer concerned with the art of submission
Rather with that of not submitting, and putting forward
Various proposals of an earthly nature, and beseeching men
    to shake off
Their human tormentors, we too believe that to those
Who in face of the approaching bomber squadrons of
    Capital go on asking too long
How we propose to do this, and how we envisage that
And what will become of their savings and Sunday trousers
    after a revolution
We have nothing much to say.


## TO A PORTABLE RADIO

You little box I carried on that trip
Concerned to save your works from getting broken
Fleeing from house to train, from train to ship
So I might hear the hated jargon spoken

Beside my bedside and to give me pain
Last thing at night, once more as dawn appears
Charting their victories, voicing my worst fears:
Promise at least you won't go dead again!

## CONCERNING THE LABEL EMIGRANT

I always found the name false which they gave us:
       Emigrants.
That means those who leave their country. But we
Did not leave, of our own free will
Choosing another land. Nor did we enter
Into a land, to stay there, if possible for ever.
Merely, we fled. We are driven out, banned.
Not a home, but an exile, shall the land be that took us in.
Restlessly we wait thus, as near as we can to the frontier
Awaiting the day of return, every smallest alteration
Observing beyond the boundary, zealously asking
Every arrival, forgetting nothing and giving up nothing
And also not forgiving anything which happened, forgiving
       nothing.
Ah, the silence of the Sound does not deceive us! We hear
       the shrieks
From their camps even here. Yes, we ourselves
Are almost like rumours of crimes, which escaped
Over the frontier. Every one of us
Who with torn shoes walks through the crowd
Bears witness to the shame which now defiles our land.
But none of us
Will stay here. The final word
Is yet unspoken.


## THOUGHTS ON THE DURATION OF EXILE

I
Don't knock any nails into the wall
Throw your coat on the chair.
What use is planning for next week?
Tomorrow you go back home.

Leave the little tree without water.
What's the point of planting trees now?
Before it's grown half as high as your doorstep
You'll have finished with here.

Put your cap across your face when you see people
          approaching.
What's the point of thumbing through foreign grammars?
The news that calls you home
Is surely in a familiar language.

Just like the flaking of old whitewash
(Do nothing to stop it!)
So too the barrier of force will crumble
That has been set up at the frontier
Keeping the rule of justice out.


II
Here's the wall, you see the nail that you hammered into it:
When, d'you think, will you be going back?
Do you want to know what you really believe?
Day by day
You're at work, seated in your study, writing.
Do you want to know what you really think of your work?
Look at the little chestnut tree
You carried a full can of water to.


SPRING 1938

I
Easter day a cold wind blew
And a flurry of snow swept over the island.
In among burgeoning hedges it lay.
My teenage son dragged me out
To save a little apricot tree up against the house

Putting aside a verse
In which I'd done the best I could
To expose that group of men
Who were preparing the holocaust
Which would lay waste our continent, and this island, my
     people
Likewise my family and me, and wipe us out.
Silently we wrapped a sack
Round the shivering tree.


II
Above the Sound hang rainclouds, but the garden is
Gilded still by the sun. The pear trees
Have green leaves and no blossom yet, the cherries
Blossom and no leaves yet. The white clusters
Seem to sprout from withered branches.
Across the wrinkled waters of the Sound
Goes a little boat with a patched sail.
The starlings' twittering
Is broken by the distant thunder
Of naval gunfire from the war games
Of the Third Reich.


III
In the willows by the Sound
Of a springtime night one often hears the screech-owl.
There's a peasant superstition that
The screech-owl is there to give men a warning
They won't live much longer. I
Who am well aware that I will have told the truth
About those in power, do not really need
To hear this from a bird.

THE CHERRY THIEF

Early the other morning, long before it was light
I was woken up to hear whistling outside my window
From up my cherry tree. Twilight was filling the garden.
There I saw a youth with a patch in his pants
Cheerfully plucking my cherries. He noticed me
Gave me a nod, and with both hands
Started stuffing cherries from the tree into all his pockets.
For quite a moment longer, when I'd once again got into my
       bed
I could hear him give his gay little whistle.

BAD TIME FOR POETRY

Yes, I know: only the happy man
Is liked. His voice
Is good to hear. His face is handsome.

The crippled tree in the yard
Shows that the soil is poor, yet
The passers-by abuse it for being crippled
And rightly so.

The green boats and the dancing sails on the Sound
Go unseen. Of it all
I see only the torn nets of the fishermen.
Why do I only record
That a village woman aged forty walks with a stoop?
The girls' breasts
Are as warm as ever.

In my poetry a rhyme
Would seem to me almost insolent.

Inside me contend
Delight at the apple tree in blossom
And horror at the house-painter's speeches.
But only the second
Drives me to my desk.


## REPORT ON A CASTAWAY

When the castaway set foot on our island
He came like one who has reached his goal.
I almost believe that when he sighted us
Who had run up to help him
He at once felt pity for us.
From the very beginning
He concerned himself with our affairs only.
Using the lessons of his shipwreck
He taught us to sail. Courage even
He instilled in us. Of the stormy waters
He spoke with great respect, doubtless
Because they had defeated a man like him. In doing so
They had of course revealed many of their tricks. This
Knowledge, he said, would make us, his pupils
Better men. Since he missed certain dishes
He improved our cooking.
Though visibly dissatisfied with himself
He was not for a moment satisfied with the state of affairs.
Surrounding himself and us. But never
In all the time he spent with us
Did we hear him complain of anyone but himself.
He died of an old wound. Even as he lay on his back he
Was testing a new knot for our fishing nets. Thus
He died learning.

SWEDISH LANDSCAPE

Beneath the grey pine trees a crumbling house.
Amid rubble a white-lacquered chest.
An altar? A counter? That is the question.
Was the body of Jesus sold here? His blood
On draught? Or linen celebrated, and boots?
Was earthly or heavenly profit made here?
Did clerics trade here or tradesmen preach?
God's lovely creation, the pine trees
Are sold off by the locksmith next door.


THE PIPES

Abandoning, in haste to cross the border
My books to friends, I left my poem too
But took along my pipes, which broke the general order
For refugees: Best have no things with you.

Those books don't mean much to the man who grim-
ly waits to see his torturers approaching.
His leather pouch and other gear for smoking
Now look like being of more use to him.


THE SON

My teenage son has asked: Should I study mathematics?
What for? I feel like saying. That two pieces of bread are
          more than one piece:
You will grasp that anyway.
My teenage son has asked: Should I study English?
What for? I feel like saying.
That empire is finished.
So all you need do is rub a hand across your belly, groaning.
Then they're sure to understand you.

My teenage son has asked: Should I study history?
What for? I feel like saying.
Better learn to stick your head in the sand like an ostrich
Then you might have a chance of living.

Yes! Study mathematics, I say
Study English, yes, study history!


EARLY ON I LEARNED

Early on I learned to change everything quickly
The ground on which I walked, the air I was breathing
Lightly I do so, yet still I see
How others want to take too much with them.
   Leave your ship light, leave lightly behind
   Leave too your ship lightly behind when they tell you
   To take the road inland.

You cannot be happy if you want to keep too much with
            you
Nor if you want what too many people do not want
Be wise, do not try to have your own way
But learn to grasp things as you pass by.
   Leave your ship light, leave lightly behind
   Leave too your ship lightly behind when they tell you
   To take the road inland.


MOTTO

So that's the lot. It's not enough, I know
Yet it might serve to tell you this is me.
I'm like the man who took a brick to show
How beautiful his house used once to be.

## MOTHER COURAGE'S SONG

You captains, tell the drums to slacken
And give your infanteers a break:
It's Mother Courage with her waggon
Full of the finest boots they make.
With crawling lice and looted cattle
With lumbering guns and straggling kit –
How can you flog them into battle
Until you get them boots that fit?
 The New Year's come. The watchmen shout.
 The thaw begins. The dead remain.
 Wherever life has not died out
 It staggers to its feet again.

Captains, how can you make them face it
March to their death without a brew?
Courage has rum with which to lace it
And boil their souls and bodies through.
Their muskets primed, their stomachs hollow
Captains, your men don't look too well.
So feed them up, and they will follow
And let you lead them into hell.
 The New Year's come. The watchmen shout.
 The thaw begins. The dead remain.
 Wherever life has not died out
 It staggers to its feet again.

And if you feel your forces fading
You won't be there to share the fruits.
For what is war but market trading
Which deals in blood instead of boots?
And some I saw dig six feet under
In haste to lie down and pass out.
Now they're at rest perhaps they wonder
Just what was all their haste about.

From Ulm to Metz, from Metz to Munich
Courage will see the war gets fed.
The war will show a well-filled tunic
Given its daily shot of lead.
But lead alone won't really nourish:
War must have soldiers to subsist.
It's you it needs to make it flourish.
The war is hungry. So enlist!

With all its luck and all its danger
This war is dragging on a bit.
Another hundred years or longer:
The common man won't benefit.
Filthy his food, no soap to shave him
The regiment steals half his pay.
But still a miracle may save him:
Tomorrow is another day!
 The New Year's come. The watchmen shout.
 The thaw begins. The dead remain.
 Wherever life has not died out
 It staggers to its feet again.


SONG OF THE SMOKE

*The Grandfather*:
 Once I believed intelligence would aid me
 I was an optimist when I was younger
 Now that I'm old I see it hasn't paid me:
 How can intelligence compete with hunger?
  And so I said: drop it!
  Like smoke twisting grey
  Into ever colder coldness, you'll
  Blow away.

*The Man*:
    I saw the conscientious man get nowhere
    And so I tried the crooked path instead
    But crookedness makes our sort travel slower.
    There seems to be no way to get ahead.
        Likewise I say: drop it!
        Like smoke twisting grey
        Into ever colder coldness, you'll
        Blow away.

*The Niece*:
    The old, they say, find little fun in hoping.
    Time's what they need, and time begins to press.
    But for the young, they say, the gates are open.
    They open, so they say, on nothingness.
        And I too say: drop it!
        Like smoke twisting grey
        Into ever colder coldness, you'll
        Blow away.


ON SUICIDE

In such a country and at such a time
There should be fewer melancholy evenings
And lofty bridges over the rivers
While the hours that link the night to morning
And the winter season too each year, are full of danger.
For, having seen all this misery
People won't linger
But will decide at once
To fling their too heavy life away.

## SONG OF THE MOLDAU

Deep down in the Moldau the pebbles are shifting
In Prague three dead emperors moulder away.
The top won't stay top, for the bottom is lifting.
The night has twelve hours, and then comes the day.

But time can't be halted. The boundless ambition
Of those now in power is running its course.
Like bloodspattered cocks they will fight for position
But time can't be halted. Not even by force.

Deep down in the Moldau the pebbles are shifting
In Prague three dead emperors moulder away.
The top won't stay top, for the bottom is lifting.
The night has twelve hours, and then comes the day.


## HE WHO WEARS THE SHOES OF GOLD

He who wears the shoes of gold
Tramples on the weak and old
Does evil all day long
And mocks at wrong.

O to carry as one's own
Heavy is the heart of stone.
The power to do ill
Wears out the will.

Hunger he will dread
Not those who go unfed:
Fear the fall of night
But not the light.

BALLAD OF KNOWLEDGE

The stupid man may work in a great hurry
But what he wants won't come from hurrying
And what he has stays with him: i.e. worry.
The trouble is: he doesn't know a thing.
The man without a horse gets trampled under
The man with one gets where he wants to go.
For knowledge helps in any job. No wonder.
You'll never get your cut, unless you know.

'Your shop's too small,' I hear my friends maintaining
'Some bigger shark is sure to swallow you.'
I clutch at those few hairs I have remaining
And wonder how to be a big shark too.
Humble myself, I know how hard the humble
Have always worked for crusts and the odd blow
So I sit tight and count my cash, and mumble:
'I'm sure to get my cut, because I know.'

For instance, take a man with kidney trouble:
He sees a specialist who tests his pee.
The patient leaves the surgery bent double
But having paid. The doctor knows, you see.
He knows it by its textbook definition –
He knows too how the scale of charges goes.
Those who don't know can die of their condition
But Doctor get his cut because he knows.

Love is a game in which one gains or loses
The lover, the beloved: who gets the breaks?
The one gets honey and the other bruises
One does the giving and the other takes.
Conceal your face, then, when you feel it flushing.
And hide your bosom if the bruising shows.
Give him a knife, he'll stab you till you're gushing
Love tells him where to cut. You see: he knows.

## LANDSCAPE OF EXILE

I, as a passenger on that last boat
Could see the gaiety of the dawn through the ropes
And how the dolphins' grey-coloured bodies leapt up
Out of the Japanese Sea.

The little horsecarts, brilliantly gilded
The pink sleeves that are worn by the matrons
In the alleyways of targeted Manila
Heightened the fugitive's pleasure.

Likewise the oil derricks and the sweet-scented gardens of
      Los Angeles
And the shadowy ravines of California could
Not leave the envoy of tragedy cold.


## DELIVER THE GOODS

Again and again
As I walk through their cities
Seeking a living, I am told:
Show us what you're made of
Lay it on the table!
Deliver the goods!
Say something to inspire us!
Tell us of our own greatness!
Divine our secret desires!
Show us the way out
Make yourself useful!
Deliver the goods!

Stand alongside us, so that
You tower over us
Show that you are one of us.

We'll make you our hero.
We can pay too, we have the wherewithal –
No one else has.
Deliver the goods!

Know that our great showmen
Are those who show what we want to have shown.
Dominate by serving us!
Endure by winning duration for us
Play our game, we'll share the loot
Deliver the goods! Be straight with us!
Deliver the goods.

When I look into their decomposing faces
My hunger disappears.


ON THINKING ABOUT HELL

On thinking about Hell, I gather
My brother Shelley found it was a place
Much like the city of London. I
Who live in Los Angeles and not in London
Find, on thinking about Hell, that it must be
Still more like Los Angeles.

In Hell too
There are, I've no doubt, these luxuriant gardens
With flowers as big as trees, which of course wither
Unhesitantly if not nourished with very expensive water.
        And fruit markets
With great heaps of fruit, albeit having
Neither smell nor taste. And endless processions of cars
Lighter than their own shadows, faster than
Mad thoughts, gleaming vehicles in which
Jolly-looking people come from nowhere and are nowhere
        bound.

And houses, built for happy people, therefore standing
    empty
Even when lived in.

The houses in Hell, too, are not all ugly.
But the fear of being thrown on the street
Wears down the inhabitants of the villas no less than
The inhabitants of the shanty towns.


## SUMMER 1942

Day after day
I see the fig trees in the garden
The rosy faces of the dealers who buy lies
The chessmen on the corner table
And the newspapers with their reports
Of bloodbaths in the Soviet Union.


## THE FISHING-TACKLE

In my room, on the whitewashed wall
Hangs a short bamboo stick bound with cord
With an iron hook designed
To snag fishing-nets from the water. The stick
Came from a second-hand store downtown. My son
Gave it to me for my birthday. It is worn.
In salt water the hook's rust has eaten through the binding.
These traces of use and of work
Lend great dignity to the stick. I
Like to think that this fishing-tackle
Was left behind by those Japanese fishermen
Whom they have now driven from the West Coast into
    camps
As suspect aliens; that it came into my hands
To keep me in mind of so many

Unsolved but not insoluble
Questions of humanity.

FIVE HOLLYWOOD ELEGIES

I

Underneath the green pepper trees, daily
The composers are on the beat, two by two
With the writers. Bach
Writes concertos for the strumpet. Dante wriggles
His shrivelled arsehole.


II

This town was christened after the angels
And you come across angels there on all sides.
They all smell of oil, and each one wears a golden pessary
And with deep blue rings all round their eyes
They take good care to feed the writers in
Their swimming pools before breakfast.


III

Every morning, to start earning my bread
I visit the market where lies are bought and sold.
Full of hope, I take my place there
With the other sellers.


IV

This city
Has made me realise:
Paradise and hell-fire
Are the same city.
For the unsuccessful
Paradise itself
Serves as hell-fire.

V

In the hills are the gold prospectors. By the sea
You come upon oil. Greater fortunes far
Are won from those dreams of happiness
Which are kept on celluloid spools.


THE LAST ELEGY

Above the four cities the fighter planes
Of the Defense Department
Circle at great heights. No doubt this
Is so that the stink of greed and of misery
Cannot manage to reach them.


HOLLYWOOD ELEGY NO. 7 (THE SWAMP)

I saw many friends and the friend I loved the most among
        them
Helplessly sunk into the swamp
I pass by daily.

And a drowning was not over
In a single morning.
This made it more terrible.
And the memory of our long talks
About the swamp, which already
Held so many powerless.

Now I watched him leaning back
Covered with leeches
In the shimmering
Softly moving slime:
Upon the sinking face
The ghastly
Blissful smile.

I, THE SURVIVOR

I know of course: it's simply luck
That I've survived so many friends. But last night in a dream
I heard those friends say of me: 'Survival of the fittest'
And I hated myself.


PROLOGUE TO THE AMERICAN GALILEO

Respected public of the way called Broad –
Tonight we're asking you to step on board
Our world of curves and measurements, where you'll
          descry
The newborn physics in their infancy.
Here you will see the life of the great Galileo Galilei.
The law of falling bodies versus the Gratias Dei
Science's fight against the rulers, put on stage
At the beginning of the modern age.
Here you'll see science in its blooming youth
Also its first compromises with the truth.
The Good, so far, has not been turned to goods
But already there's something nasty in the woods
Which stops that truth from reaching the majority
And won't relieve, but aggravate their poverty.
We think such sights are relevant today
The modern age is quick to pass away.
We hope you'll lend a charitable ear
To what we say, since otherwise we fear
If you won't learn from Galileo's experience
The Bomb will put in a personal appearance.

LIGHT AS THOUGH NEVER TOUCHING THE FLOOR

Light as though never touching the floor and obeying
Phantasmal drumming the two unfortunate princely
    brothers
Came on to the stage and duly began
To be there on the light-encircled boards. And the distances
Remained agreeable between the groups and whirring like
    knives
Infallible and quivering in the bull's-eye
The sentences came, but grouping and cadence
Hung between long memorised chance and half-
Forgotten design. Quickly the guard was chosen
The spy engaged, the thinker hired and, pained
With frozen smiles, the Court heard the princely brothers
Exhort their sister urgently to be chaste, recommend
Virginity to the beautiful girl. Brief farewell. Refused
Is the embrace never offered. Alone
Stands the chaste one, abjuring
Chastity.


THE FRIENDS

The war separated
Me, the writer of plays, from my friend the stage designer.
The cities where we worked are no longer there.
When I walk through the cities that still are
At times I say: that blue piece of washing
My friend would have placed it better.


THE LIGHTING

Give us some light on the stage, electrician. How can we
Playwrights and actors put forward
Our images of the world in half darkness? The dim twilight

Induces sleep. But we need the audience's
Wakeful-, even watchfulness. Let them
Do their dreaming in the light. The little bit of night
We now and then require can be
Indicated by moons or lamps, likewise our acting
Can make clear what time of day it is
Whenever needed. The Elizabethan wrote us verses
About a heath at evening
Which no electrician can match, nor even
The heath itself. So light up
What we have laboured over, that the audience
Can see how the outraged peasant woman
Sits down on the Finnish soil
As if it belonged to her.

## THE CURTAINS

On the big curtain paint the cantankerous
Peace dove of my brother Picasso. Behind it
Stretch the wire rope and hang
My lightly fluttering half curtains
Which cross like two waves of foam to make
The working woman handing out pamphlets
And the recanting Galileo both disappear.
Following the change of plays they can be
Of rough linen or of silk
Or of white leather or of red, and so on.
Only don't make them too dark, for on them
You must project the titles of the following
Incidents, for the sake of tension and that
The right thing may be expected. And please make
My curtain half-height, don't block the stage off.
Leaning back, let the spectator
Notice the busy preparations being so
Ingeniously made for him, a tin moon is
Seen swinging down, a shingle roof

Is carried in; don't show him too much
But show something. And let him observe
That this is not magic but
Work, my friends.


WEIGEL'S PROPS

Just as the millet farmer picks out for his trial plot
The heaviest seeds and the poet
The exact words for his verse so
She selects the objects to accompany
Her characters across the stage. The pewter spoon
Which Courage sticks
In the lapel of her Mongolian jacket, the party card
For warm-hearted Vlassova and the fishing net
For the other, Spanish mother or the bronze bowl
For dust-gathering Antigone. Impossible to confuse
The split bag which the working woman carries
For her son's leaflets, with the moneybag
Of the keen tradeswoman. Each item
In her stock is hand picked: straps and belts
Pewter boxes and ammunition pouches; hand picked too
The chicken and the stick which at the end
The old woman twists through the draw-rope
The Basque woman's board on which she bakes her bread
And the Greek woman's board of shame, strapped to her
        back
With holes for her hands to stick through, the Russian's
Jar of lard, so small in the policeman's hand; all
Selected for age, function and beauty
By the eyes of the knowing
The hands of the bread-baking, net-weaving
Soup-cooking connoisseur
Of reality.

THE ANACHRONISTIC PROCESSION
OR
FREEDOM AND DEMOCRACY

Spring returned to Germany.
In the ruins you could see
Early green birch buds unfold
Graceful, tentative and bold

As from many a southern valley
Voters left their houses to rally
Forming a disjointed column
Underneath two banners solemn

Whose supports were all worm-eaten
Their inscription weatherbeaten
Though its gist appeared to be
Freedom and Democracy.

Every church bell started ringing.
Soldiers' widows, airmen's women
Orphaned, shell-shocked, crippled, raped
Open-mouthed the watchers gaped.

And the deaf could tell the blind
Who it was that marched behind
Such a slogan as, maybe
Freedom and Democracy.

At the head a featherbrain
Sang with all his might and main:
'Allons, enfants, God save the King
And the dollar, ting-a-ling.'

Next, with monstrance held up high
Two in monkish garb strode by.
As for what they wore below –
Did I glimpse a jack-boot's toe?

On their flag the cross looked thicker
Than the previous swastika.
Since the latter's now outdated
It had been obliterated.

Under this there marched a father
Sent from Rome, where (so we gather)
He had left His Holiness
Gazing East in deep distress.

Next to celebrate the Night
Of the Long Knives, comes a tight
Knot of men who loudly call
For another free-for-all.

Then the faceless trust directors
Those men's patrons and protectors:
Pray, for our arms industry
Freedom and Democracy!

Like a cock worn out with rutting
A Pan-German passes, strutting
He wants Freedom of the Word (a
Word like 'Murder').

Keeping step, next march the teachers
Toadying, brain-corrupting creatures
For the right to educate
Boys to butchery and hate.

Then the medical advisers
Hitler's slaves, mankind's despisers
Asking, might they now select
A few Reds to vivisect.

Three grim dons, whose reputation
Rests on mass extermination
Stake their claim for chemistry:
Freedom and Democracy.

Next our whitewashed Nazi friends
On whom the new State depends:
Body lice, whose pet preserve is
In the higher civil service.

After them behold the former
Editors of Streicher's *Stürmer*
All set to protest unless
We get Freedom of the Press.

Next in line, honest taxpayers
Once renowned as semite-slayers
Gagged today, want guarantees
For the new minorities.

As for those parliamentarians
Who in Hitler's day were Aryans
And now pose as barristers:
Freedom for such gifts as theirs!

While the black-market man, asked
Why he came out on the march
Unconditionally replies:
To preserve free enterprise.

And the judge (now this is rich)
Wields outmoded laws by which
Hitlerised up to the hilt, he
Finds men like himself not guilty.

Poets, painters and musicians
Seeking grub and good positions
Noble souls, who now assure us
They were no friends of the Führer's.

Through the streets resounds the lash:
SS men flogging for cash.
Freedom needs them too, you see –
Freedom and Democracy.

And those Nazi women there
With their skirts up in the air –
Legs, they reckon, are what gets
Allied sweets and cigarettes.

Strength-through-joy dames, spies, Jew-baiters
Gestapo investigators
Tax-gifts-interest stimulators
Irredentist liberators

Blood and dirt, elective allies
Winding over hills and valleys
Belched, stank, squittered out their plea:
Freedom and Democracy!

Till, all stinking fit to burst
They arrived in Munich, first
City of the Nazi Movement
Home of German self-entombment.

Misinformed, in misery
See its baffled bourgeoisie
Standing where their houses stood
Lacking certainties and food.

As the smelly column staggers
Through the rubble with its banners
By the Brown House there's a surge
And six silent shades emerge.

All now halt to mark this meeting
And the six, heads bared in greeting
Join the column which once more
Bears its banners on before.

In six cars those six assorted
Party members are transported
While the crowd shouts: Now we'll see
Freedom and Democracy.

Bony hand grasping a whip
First OPPRESSION takes a trip
In a half-track furnished free
By our heavy industry.

In a rusty tank, much greeted
Next comes PLAGUE. His breath is foetid.
To conceal his flaking skin
He wraps a brown scarf round his chin.

After him see FRAUD appear
Brandishing a jug of beer.
You will get your glasses filled when
You have let him take your children.

Older than the hills, and yet
Still out for what she can get
STUPIDITY staggers on board
Riveted she stares at Fraud.

Lolling back, as at a play
MURDER too is on his way
Perfectly at ease as he
Hums: Sweet dream of liberty.

Shaken by the latest crises
ROBBERY materialises
In Field-Marshal's uniform
With the globe beneath his arm.

Each of these six grisly figures
Firmly based, with ready triggers
Says that there has got to be
Freedom and Democracy.

Lurching, a huge hearse comes last
Once those six monsters have passed
Inside which, unseen and wretched
Who can tell what race lies stretched?

Cold winds blow a requiem
From the ruins over them
Former tenants of the flats
That once stood here. Then great rats

Leave the rubble in their masses
Join the column as it passes
Squeaking 'Freedom!' as they flee
'Freedom and Democracy!'

HOMECOMING

My native town: what will it look like?
Guided by bomber squadrons
I shall come home.
Where will it lie? There, where those mountainous
Pinnacles of smoke stand.
There, in the furnace. That
Is it.

My native town: then how will it greet me?
Before me go the bombers. Death-dealing locusts
Tell you I shall be coming.
Conflagrations
Hail the son's return.


WAR HAS BEEN GIVEN A BAD NAME

I am told that the best people have begun saying
How, from a moral point of view, the Second World War
Fell below the standard of the First. The Wehrmacht
Allegedly deplores the methods by which the SS effected
The extermination of certain peoples. The Ruhr
        industrialists
Are said to regret the bloody manhunts
Which filled their mines and factories with slave workers.
        The intellectuals
So I heard, condemn industry's demand for slave workers
Likewise their unfair treatment. Even the bishops
Dissociate themselves from this way of waging war; in short
        the feeling
Prevails in every quarter that the Nazis did the Fatherland
A lamentably bad turn, and that war
While in itself natural and necessary, has, thanks to the
Unduly uninhibited and positively inhuman

Way in which it was conducted on this occasion, been
Discredited for some time to come.


ENCOUNTER WITH THE POET
AUDEN

Lunching me, a kindly act
In an alehouse, still intact
He sat looming like a cloud
Over the beer-sodden crowd.

And kept harping with persistence
On the bare fact of existence
I.e., a theory built around it
Recently in France propounded.


BAD TIMES

The tree tells why it bore no fruit.
The poet tells why his lines went wrong.
The general tells why the war was lost.

Pictures, painted on brittle canvas.
Records of exploration, handed down to the forgetful.
Great behaviour, observed by no one.

Should the cracked vase be used as a pisspot?
Should the ridiculous tragedy be turned into a farce?
Should the disfigured sweetheart be put in the kitchen?

All praise to those who leave crumbling houses.
All praise to those who bar their door against a demoralised
        friend.
All praise to those who forget about the unworkable plan.

The house is built of the stones that were available.
The rebellion was raised using the rebels that were available.
The picture was painted using the colours that were
    available.

Meals were made of whatever food could be had.
Gifts were given to the needy.
Words were spoken to those who were present.
Work was done with the existing resources, wisdom and
    courage.

Carelessness should not be forgiven.
More would have been possible.
Regret is expressed.
(What good could it do?)


OBSERVATION

When I returned
My hair was not yet grey
And I was glad

The travails of the mountains lie behind us.
Before us lie the travails of the plains.


LOVE SONGS

1
After I had gone from you
That ever-present day
And once again began to see
All that I saw were gay.

Since we passed that evening hour
You know the one I mean
My legs are nimbler by far
My mouth is more serene.

And since I felt so, tree and bush
And meadow grow more greenly
The very water when I wash
Flows over me more coolly.


II
*Song of a Loving Woman*

When you delight me
Then I think sometimes:
If I could die now
I would be happy
Till my life's end.

Then when you are old
And you think of me
I shall look as now
You'll have a sweetheart
That is still young.


III
Seven roses on the bush
Six belong to the wind
One will stay there, so there's just
One for me to find.

Seven times I'll summon you
Six times stay away
But the seventh, promise me
Come without delay.


IV
My dearest one gave me a branch
The leaves on it are brown.

The year is drawing to its close
Our love is just begun.


THE SOLUTION

After the uprising of the 17th June
The Secretary of the Writers' Union
Had leaflets distributed in the Stalinallee
Stating that the people
Had forfeited the confidence of the government
And could win it back only
By redoubled efforts. Would it not be easier
In that case for the government
To dissolve the people
And elect another?


CHANGING THE WHEEL

I sit by the roadside
The driver changes the wheel.
I do not like the place I have come from.
I do not like the place I am going to.
Why with impatience do I
Watch him changing the wheel?

NASTY MORNING

The silver poplar, a celebrated local beauty
Today an old harridan. The lake
A puddle of dish-water, don't touch!
The fuchsias amongst the snapdragon cheap and vain.
Why?
Last night in a dream I saw fingers pointing at me
As at a leper. They were worn with toil and
They were broken.

You don't know! I shrieked
Conscience-stricken.


STILL AT IT

The plates are slammed down so hard
The soup slops over.
In shrill tones
Resounds the order: Now eat!

The Prussian eagle
Jabbing food down
The gullets of its young.


HOT DAY

Hot day. My writing-case on my knee
I sit in the summer-house. A green boat
Appears through the willow. In the stern
A stout nun, stoutly clad. In front of her
An elderly person in a bathing-costume, probably a priest.
At the oars, rowing for all he's worth
A child. Just like old times, I think
Just like old times.

THE SMOKE

The little house among trees by the lake.
From the roof smoke rises.
Without it
How dreary would be
House, trees and lake.

IRON

In a dream last night
I saw a great storm.
It seized the scaffolding
It tore the cross-clasps
The iron ones, down.
But what was made of wood
Swayed and remained.

THE ONE-ARMED MAN IN THE UNDERGROWTH

Dripping with sweat, he bends down
To gather brushwood. The mosquitoes
He fends off with shakes of the head. Between his knees
He laboriously bundles his firewood. Groaning
He straightens himself, holds up his hand to feel
If it's raining. Hand upraised
The dreaded SS man.

EIGHT YEARS AGO

There was a time
When all was different here.
The butcher's wife knows.
The postman has too erect a gait.
And what was the electrician?

READING HORACE

Even the Flood
Did not last for ever.
There came a time
When the black waters ebbed.
Yes, but how few
Have lasted longer.

THIS SUMMER'S SKY

High above the lake a bomber flies.
From the rowing boats
Children look up, women, an old man. From a distance
They appear like young starlings, their beaks
Wide open for food.

THE TROWEL

In a dream I stood on a building site. I was
A bricklayer. In my hand
I held a trowel. But when I bent down
For mortar, a shot rang out
That tore half the iron
Off my trowel.

## READING A LATE GREEK POET

At the time when their fall was certain –
On the ramparts the lament for the dead had begun –
The Trojans adjusted small pieces, small pieces
In the triple wooden gates, small pieces.
And began to take courage, to hope.

The Trojans too, then.


## THE ABANDONED GREENHOUSE

Exhausted from watering the fruit trees
I lately stepped through the open door into the small
    greenhouse
Where in the shadow of the tattered blind
Lie the remains of the rare flowers.

Still, made from wood, cloth and wire netting, stands
The installation, still the twine holds
The pale withered stems upright.
Bygone days' attention
Is still visible, many a subtle touch. Across the tented roof
Sways the shadow of the common evergreens
Which, living by rain, have no need of art.
As always the lovely and sensitive
Are no longer.

## THE LITTLE ROSE, OH HOW SHOULD IT BE LISTED?

The little rose, oh how should it be listed?
Suddenly dark red and young and near?
Oh we never knew that it existed
Then we came, and saw that it was there.

Unexpected till we came and saw it
Unbelievable as soon as seen
Hit the mark, despite not aiming for it:
Isn't that how things have always been?

## PRAISE OF THE USSR

All the world was telling of
Our misfortune.
But still there sat at our
Bare board
The hope of the numberless exploited which
Lives on water alone.
And our teacher was Knowledge, who
Behind our broken-down door
Gave clear lessons to all those present.
Once the door's been broken, we
Sit on inside, plainly visible
Whom no frost can kill off, nor hunger
Ever tireless, debating
The future of the world.

## THE INTERNATIONALE

Comrades report:
In the foothills of the Pamir
We met a woman in charge of a small cocoon farm
Who has convulsions whenever she hears the
Internationale. She told her story:
In the civil war her husband was
The leader of a band of partisans. Gravely wounded
Lying in their hut, he was betrayed. Taking him captive
The White Guards cried: You won't be singing your
Internationale much longer! And before his eyes
They seized his wife and raped her on the bed.
Then the man began to sing.
And he sang the Internationale
Even when they shot his youngest child
And he ceased singing
When they took and shot his son
And he ceased living. Since that day
The woman says, she has had convulsions
When she hears the Internationale.
And, she tells us, it has been very hard
To find a place to work in any of the Soviet republics
Where one doesn't hear the song sung
For from Moscow to the Pamir
These days you can't escape the sound of
The Internationale. But it is heard less often
In the Pamir.
And we continued talking of her work.
She told us: So far the district
Has only half fulfilled the Plan.
But her locality is already quite transformed
Unrecognisable, it yet grows daily more familiar
A new crowd of people is providing
New work, new leisure
And by next year it is likely
The Plan will be exceeded

And once this happens, then they'll build
A factory here: once that is built
Well, she said, on that day I shall
Sing the Internationale.


WASHING
(C.N.)

When years ago I showed you
How to wash first thing in the morning
With bits of ice in the water
Of the little copper bowl
Immersing your face, your eyes open
Then, while you dried yourself with the rough towel
Reading the difficult lines of your part
From the sheet pinned to the wall, I said:
That's something you're doing for yourself; make it
Exemplary.

Now I hear that you are said to be in prison.
The letters I wrote on your behalf
Remained unanswered. The friends I approached for you
Are silent. I can do nothing for you. What
Will your morning bring? Will you still do something for
        yourself?
Hopeful and responsible
With good movements, exemplary?


IS THE PEOPLE INFALLIBLE?

I
My teacher
Tall and kindly
Has been shot, condemned by a people's court
As a spy. His name is damned.

His books are destroyed. Talk about him
Is suspect and suppressed.
Suppose he is innocent?


2
The sons of the people have found him guilty
The factories and collective farms of the workers
The world's most heroic institutions
Have identified him as an enemy.
No voice has been raised for him.
Suppose he is innocent?


3
The people has many enemies.
In the highest places
Sit enemies. In the most useful laboratories
Sit enemies. They build
Dykes and canals for the good of whole continents, and the
        canals
Silt up and the dykes
Collapse. The man in charge has to be shot.
Suppose he is innocent?


4
The enemy goes disguised.
He pulls a workman's cap over his eyes. His friends
Know him as a conscientious worker. His wife
Shows his leaky shoes
Worn out in the people's service.
And yet he is an enemy. Was my teacher one of them?
Suppose he is innocent?


5
To speak of the enemies that may be sitting in the people's
        courts
Is dangerous, for courts have reputations to keep up.
To ask for papers proving guilt in black and white

Is senseless, for there need be no such papers.
The criminals have proofs of their innocence to hand.
The innocent often have no proof.
Is it best to keep silent then?
Suppose he is innocent?

6
What 5000 have built one man can destroy.
Of 50 condemned
One may be guiltless.
Suppose he is innocent?

7
Suppose he is innocent
How will he go to his death?

THE WEIGHTS ON THE SCALES

The weights on the scales
Are great. Thrown into the other pan
Is shrewdness
And, as a necessary makeweight
Cruelty.

The worshippers look around:
What was wrong? The god?
Or the worship?

But the machines?
But the victory trophies?
But the child with no bread?
But the bleeding comrade's
Unheard scream of terror?

He who commanded everything
Did not do everything.

Promised were apples
Undelivered was bread.


## THE GOD IS WORM-EATEN

The god is worm-eaten.
The worshippers beat their breasts
As they beat women's bottoms
With ecstasy.


## DEVELOPING A WHEAT TO STAND THE WINTER

Developing a wheat to stand the winter
Demands the engagement of many researchers.
Must the construction of socialism
Be botched together by a handful of people in the dark?

Is the Leader dragging the led
Up to a peak that he alone knows?
Statistically at least
By commission or omission
The led do the leading.


## PRIDE

When the American soldier told me
That the well fed middle class German girls
Could be bought for tobacco and the lower middle class
For chocolate
But the starved Russian slave workers could not be bought
I felt proud.

## GERMANY, YOU BLOND PALE CREATURE

Germany, you blond pale creature
With wild clouds and a gentle brow
What happened in your silent skies?
You have become the carrion pit of Europe.

Vultures over you!
Beasts tear your good body
The dying smear you with their filth
And their water
Wets your fields. Fields!

How gentle your rivers once
Now poisoned by purple anilin.
With their bare teeth children root
Your cereals up, they're
Hungry.

But the harvest floats into the
Stinking water.

Germany, you blond pale creature
Neverneverland. Full of
Departed souls. Full of dead people.
Nevermore nevermore will it beat –
Your heart, which has gone
Mouldy, which you have sold
Pickled in chili saltpetre
In exchange
For flags.

Oh carrion land, misery hole!
Shame strangles the remembrance of you
And in the young men whom
You have not ruined
America awakens.

## O GERMANY, PALE MOTHER

Let others speak of their disgrace.
I am speaking of my own.

O Germany, pale mother
How you sit defiled
Among the peoples!
Among the besmirched
You stand out.

Of your sons the poorest
Lies struck down.
When his hunger was great
Your other sons
Raised their hands against him.
This is now notorious.

With their hands thus raised
Raised against their brother
They stride around insolently before you
And laugh in your face.
This is known.

In your house
Lies are loudly bawled
But truth
Must keep silent.
Is that so?

Why do the oppressors on every side praise you, but
The oppressed indict you?
The exploited
Point their fingers at you, but
The exploiters laud the system
Devised in your house.

And at the same time all see you
Hiding the hem of your skirt, which is bloody
With the blood of your
Best son.

When they hear the speeches issuing from your house,
        people laugh.
But whoever sees you grips his knife
As on seeing a murderess.

O Germany, pale mother
What have your sons done to you
That you sit among the peoples
A mockery or a threat!


ON GERMANY

You pleasant Bavarian forests, you cities on the Main
Spruce-covered Hesse mountains and you, shadowy Black
        Forest
You shall remain.
Thuringia's reddish screes, Brandenburg's frugal scrub
You black Ruhr cities, with your traffic of iron barges, why
Should you not remain?
And you, many-citied Berlin
Busy above and below the asphalt, may remain and you
Hanseatic ports shall remain and Saxony's
Teeming towns, you shall remain and you of Silesia
Wreathed in smoke, looking east, shall remain.
Only the scum of generals, gauleiters
Only the lords of factories, stockbrokers
Only the landlords, bailiffs – these are to go.
Sky and earth and wind and all that was made by man
Can remain, but
The filth, the exploiters – that
Cannot remain.

### GERMANY (ONE STORMY NIGHT)

One stormy night, a pitch-black night
A twig produced a flower
I woke up in a sudden fright
And found the twig in flower.

The Hitler spook, that bloody spook
Will one day soon have vanished:
'The Hitlers come, the Hitlers go
Their people is not finished.'

This Hitler will be swept away
If we can work together.
And our beloved Germany
Will flower as ever.


### GERMANY 1945

Indoors is death by plague
Outdoors is death by cold.
So where are we to be?
The sow has shat in her bed
The sow's my mum. I said:
O mother mine, o mother mine
What have you done to me?


### CHILDREN'S ANTHEM

Grace spare not and spare no labour
Passion nor intelligence
That a decent German nation
Flourish as do other lands.

That the people give up flinching
At the crimes which we evoke
And hold out their hand in friendship
As they do to other folk.

Neither over nor yet under
Other peoples will we be
From the Oder to the Rhineland
From the Alps to the North Sea.

And because we'll make it better
Let us guard and love our home
Love it as our dearest country
As the others love their own.

## GERMANY 1952

O Germany, so torn in pieces
And never left alone!
The cold and dark increases
While each sees to his own.
Such lovely fields you'd have
Such cities thronged and gay;
If you'd but trust yourself
All would be child's play.

## EVERYTHING CHANGES

Everything changes. You can make
A fresh start with your final breath.
But what has happened has happened. And the water
You once poured into the wine cannot be
Drained off again.

What has happened has happened. The water
You once poured into the wine cannot be
Drained off again, but
Everything changes. You can make
A fresh start with your final breath.


ONCE

This coldness once seemed wonderful to me
And the freshness brushed life into my skin
And the bitterness tasted good, and I felt free
To dine or not according to my whim
Supposing darkness were to ask me in.

Cold was the well from which I drew my vigour
And nothingness gave me this unbounded space.
Marvellous it was when a rare brilliant flicker
Cut through the natural darkness. Short-lived? Yes.
But I, old enemy, was always quicker.


ONLY A FLEETING
GLANCE

'Only a fleeting glance
Could take her in
So it was merely chance
Made me her man.'

'Only in passing I
Entered his life
So, unregardedly
Became his wife.'

Both let the time go by
Till it was spent
Put on our overcoats
Embraced, and went.


## WHEN IN MY WHITE ROOM AT THE CHARITÉ

When in my white room at the Charité
I woke towards morning
And heard the blackbird, I understood
Better. Already for some time
I had lost all fear of death. For nothing
Can be wrong with me if I myself
Am nothing. Now
I managed to enjoy
The song of every blackbird after me too.


## AND I ALWAYS THOUGHT

And I always thought: the very simplest words
Must be enough. When I say what things are like
Everyone's heart must be torn to shreds.
That you'll go down if you don't stand up for yourself
Surely you see that.

## TO THOSE BORN LATER

### 1

Truly, I'm living in a time of darkness
When an unlined brow
Simply denotes an absence of heart. The man who laughs
Has not yet taken in
The terrifying message.

What d'you think of times when
If you start discussing oak trees it's almost criminal
As implying acquiescence in the horrors?
That man who calmly walks across the street
Is already out of reach of his friends
Who are in trouble.

They tell me: Eat and drink, enjoy what you have!
How can I think of eating and drinking, when it means
          snatching what I eat
From someone starving, and to drink water
Makes a thirsty man go short.
And yet I eat and drink still.

I would like to be wise.
In the ancient books it says what wisdom is:
Not to let the world's disputes touch you
And to use your time with no sense of panic.
Not to want things but dismiss them, let them be forgotten.
None of this can I do:
Truly, I'm living in a time of darkness.

### 2

I came to the towns in times of great confusion
When they were ruled by hunger.
I came to live with people in a time of uproar
And I began rebelling with them.

That is how I made use
Of my time on earth allotted me.

I took my mealtimes between the battles
I did my sleeping among the killers.
As for love, I was careless
And had no patience for looking at Nature.
That is how I made use
Of my time on earth allotted me.

The roads all led into a quagmire in my time.
My speech gave me away to the butchers.
There was not much that I could do. But those in power
Would have been much more at ease without me: so I liked
        to think.
That is how I made use
Of my time on earth allotted me.

Our forces weren't all that strong. Our goal
Lay right in the distance.
It was plainly visible, though I myself
Might not attain it.
That is how I made use
Of my time on earth allotted me.


3
You, who will come to the surface
Of the overwhelming deluge that covered us
Just think
When you complain about our weakness
Of those dark times
Which all of you escaped.

Yes, we went, as often changing countries as changing shoes
Through the wars of the classes, despairing
Each time we found an abuse, and no sense of outrage.

All the same we realise:
Even hatred of debasement can
Distort your features.
Even anger at injustices will
Make your voice hoarse. Oh we
Who always hoped to prepare a basis for friendliness
Never could be friendly ourselves.

You, though, when things are moving forward
So that man becomes a helper to other men
Look back on us
With indulgence.

# Notes

This is the only critical 'apparatus' to the book. It lists, from left to right across the page, the section heading, English and operative German title of each poem, its date of composition, its reference in the main Methuen editions (P for *Poems 1913–1956*, PSP for *Poems and Songs from the Plays*, blank if not included in either), page reference to significant new notes or variants in the latest German ('Berliner und Frankfurter' or BF) edition, initials of translator, initials of principal composers (b for tunes supplied by Brecht himself, br Franz Bruinier, d Paul Dessau, e Hanns Eisler, m Dominic Muldowney, w Kurt Weill) and page number in this volume. The sign # indicates that the English text has been re-translated to fit the music. The P references give page numbers, which are also those under which the notes to individual poems are listed in that book; the PSP numbers are those of poems, not pages, as used in that volume. Those notes should be consulted for references to earlier German publications. In the present book a few brief notes are appended to previously untranslated poems or in cases of additional information. A list of the principal musical settings is given on page 148.

| Title | Date | Refs | Trs | Music | Page |
|---|---|---|---|---|---|
| MARKERS | | | | | |
| Questions from a worker who reads / *Fragen eines lesenden Arbeiters* | 1935 | P252 | MH | | 1 |
| My audience / *Mein Zuschauer* | 1930s | PSP116 | JW | | 2 |
| Of all the works of man / *Von allen Werken* | 1932 | P192 | | | 2 |
| Years ago when I / *Als ich vor Jahren* | 1935 | P263 | FJ | | 3 |
| The play is over / *Aus ist das Stück* | 1943/4 | P342 | JW | m | 4 |
| THE DEAD SOLDIER | | | | | |
| Legend of the dead soldier / *Legende vom toten Soldaten* | 1918 | PSP2 | JW | b | 5 |
| FROM BRECHT'S PSALTER | | | | | |
| The first psalm / *Erster Psalm* | 1920 | P43 | CM | | 8 |
| The second psalm / *Zweiter Psalm* | 1920 | P44 | CM | | 9 |

| Title | Date | Refs | Trs | Music | Page |
|---|---|---|---|---|---|
| The fourth psalm / *Vierter Psalm* | 1920 | P77 | CM | | 10 |
| Song about my mother / *Lied von meiner Mutter* | 1920 | P40 | CM | | 11 |
| **BALLADS** | | | | | |
| Ballad of the pirates / *Ballade von den Seeräubern* | 1918 | P18 | JW | b | 12 |
| Of François Villon / *Vom François Villon* | 1918 | P16 BF13.113 | JW | | 16 |
| Ballad of Mazeppa / *Ballade vom Mazeppa* | 1922 | BF11.309, 319 | MS | | 17 |
| Ballad of the girl and the soldier / *Ballade vom Weib und dem Soldaten* | c.1922 | PSP18 | JW | d, e | 19 |
| **THE FLOW OF THINGS** | | | | | |
| Those days of my youth / *Oh! Ihr Zeiten meiner Jugend* | 1921 | P75 | JW | | 20 |
| An inscription touches off sentimental memories / *Sentimentale Erinnerung vor einer Inschrift* | 1922 | P85 | JW | | 21 |
| Remembering Marie A. / *Erinnerung an die Marie A.* | 1920 | P35 | JW | b | 22 |
| The ship / *Das Schiff* | c.1919 | P25 | JW | | 23 |
| Of poor B.B. / *Vom armen B.B.* | 1922 | BF13.241, 487 | MH | | 24 |
| **THE MAHAGONNY MYTH** | | | | | |
| Alabama song | 1925 | PSP25 | EH | b, w | 26 |
| Mahagonny song no. 1 | 1924/5 | PSP13 | JW | b, w | 27 |
| Mahagonny song no. 3 | 1924/5 | PSP15 | JW | b, w | 28 |
| Benares song | 1926 | PSP26 | EH | b, w | 30 |
| **SIX SONNETS** | | | | | |
| Discovery about a young woman / *Entdeckung an einer jungen Frau* | c.1925 | P114 | JW | | 31 |
| The opium smoker / *Die Opiumräucherin* | 1925 | P114 | JW | | 31 |
| Cow feeding / *Kuh beim Fressen* | 1925 | P115 | JW | | 32 |
| Sonnet on a new edition of François Villon / *Sonnet zur Neuausgabe des François Villon* | 1930 | P180 | JW | | 33 |
| On Dante's poems to Beatrice / *Über die Gedichte des Dante auf der Beatrice* | 1934 | P214 | JW | | 33 |
| On Shakespeare's play / *Über Shakespeares Stück Hamlet* | c.1938 | P311 | JW | | 34 |

| Title | Date | Refs | Trs | Music | Page |
|---|---|---|---|---|---|
| Ballad of good living / *Ballade vom angenehmen Leben* | 1928 | PSP41 | JW | w | 60 |
| New ending to the Ballad of Mac the Knife (film version) / *Neue Schlussstrophen* | 1931 | PSP50 | JW | w | 61 |

POLITICS OF THE THIRTIES

| | | | | | |
|---|---|---|---|---|---|
| Song of the SA man / *Das Lied vom SA-Mann* | 1931 | P191 | JW | e | 62 |
| Alter the world, it needs it / *Ändere die Welt, sie braucht es* | 1930 | PSP80 | JW | e | 63 |
| Praise of the Party / *Lob der Partei* | 1930 | PSP81 | JW | e | 63 |
| The spring / *Das Frühjahr kommt* | 1931 | PSP86 BF14.527 | JW | e | 64 |
| Solely because of the increasing disorder / *Ausschliesslich wegen* | 1937/8 | P225 | FJ | | 65 |
| Report from Germany / *Rapport von Deutschland* | c.1934 | P245 | FJ | | 66 |
| Ballad of Marie Sanders, the 'Jews' Whore' / *Ballade von der 'Judenhure' Marie Sanders* | 1935 | P251 | JW | e | 67 |
| But for the Jews advising against it / *Wenn die Juden es ihm nicht abrieten* | 1934/5 | BF14.286, 609 | MM | | 68 |
| Letter to Theatre Union / *Brief an das Arbeitertheater 'Theatre Union'* | 1935 | PSP109 | JW | | 69 |

THEATRE POEMS

| | | | | | |
|---|---|---|---|---|---|
| The playwright's song / *Lied des Stückeschreibers* | 1935 | P257 BF14.613 | JW | | 73 |
| The moment before impact / *Der Nachschlag* | c.1938 | P342 | EA | m | 75 |
| Letter to the playwright Odets / *Brief an den Stückeschreiber Odets* | 1936 | P260 | MH | | 76 |
| The actress in exile / *Die Schauspielerin im Exil* | 1937 | BF14.355 | JW | | 76 |
| An actress soliloquises while making up / *Selbstgespräch einer Schauspielerin beim Schminken* | c.1938 | BF14.423, 671 | MM | | 77 |

FIVE SONNETS

| | | | | | |
|---|---|---|---|---|---|
| Emigrant's lament / *Klage des Emigranten* | 1939 | P306 BF14.678 | ER | | 78 |
| Sonnet no. 19 / *Sonett Nr. 19* | 1939 | P330 | JW | | 79 |
| Sonnet no. 1 / *Sonett Nr. 1* | 1939 | P345 | JW | | 79 |
| Finnish landscape / *Finnische Landschaft* | 1940 | P353 | JW | e | 80 |

| Title | Date | Refs | Trs | Music | Page |
|---|---|---|---|---|---|
| In favour of a long, broad skirt / *Empfehlung eines langen, weiten Rocks* | *c.*1944 | P398 | JW | | 80 |

VISIONS

| | | | | | |
|---|---|---|---|---|---|
| Parade of the Old New / *Parade des alten Neuen* | 1939 | P323 | JW | | 81 |
| Great Babel gives birth / *Die Niederkunft der grossen Babel* | *c.*1938 | P324 | JW | | 82 |
| Roll-call of the virtues and the vices / *Appell der Laster und Tugenden* | *c.*1939 | PSP122 | JW | | 82 |

NORTHERN EXILE

| | | | | | |
|---|---|---|---|---|---|
| The Buddha's parable of the burning house / *Gleichnis des Buddha vom brennenden Haus* | 1937 | P290 | MH | | 85 |
| To a portable radio / *Auf den kleinen Radioapparat* | 1940 | P351 | JW | e | 86 |
| Concerning the label Emigrant / *Über die Bezeichnung Emigranten* | 1937 | P301 | SS | | 87 |
| Thoughts on the duration of exile / *Gedanken über die Dauer des Exils* | *c.*1937 | P301 | CM | e | 87 |
| Spring 1938 / *Frühling 1938* (Includes 'Easter Sunday' and 'The death-bird') | 1938 | P303f | JW# | e | 88 |
| The cherry thief / *Der Kirschdieb* | 1938 | P304 | JW# | e | 90 |
| Bad time for poetry / *Schlechte Zeit für Lyrik* | 1939 | P330 | | | 90 |
| Report on a castaway / *Bericht über einen Gescheiterten* | 1939 | P304 | FJ | | 91 |
| Swedish landscape / *Schwedische Landschaft* | 1939 | P333 | MH | | 92 |
| The pipes / *Die Pfeifen* | 1940 | P352 | JW# | e | 92 |
| The son / *Der Sohn* (1940, VI) | 1940 | P348 | JW# | e | 92 |
| Early on I learned / *Frühzeitig schon lernte ich* | 1940 | P357 | JW. | | 93 |
| Motto / *Dies ist nun alles* | 1940 | P347 | JW# | e | 93 |

FROM THE LATER PLAYS

| | | | | | |
|---|---|---|---|---|---|
| Mother Courage's song | ?1939 | PSP117 | JW- | d | 94 |
| Song of the smoke / *Das Lied vom Rauch* | ?1940 | PSP124 | JW. | d | 95 |
| On suicide / *Über den Selbstmord* | 1940 | PSP130 | JW# | d, e, m | 96 |
| Song of the Moldau / *Das Lied von der Moldau* | 1943 | PSP139 | WR | e | 97 |
| He who wears the shoes of gold / *Ginge es in goldnen Schuhen* | ?1944 | PSP150 | WHA | d | 97 |
| Ballad of knowledge / *Ballade vom Wissen* | 1936/7 | PSP112 | JW | | 98 |

| Title | Date | Refs | Trs | Music | Page |
|---|---|---|---|---|---|
| **CALIFORNIA EXILE** | | | | | |
| Landscape of exile / *Landschaft des Exils* | 1941 | P363 BF15.365 | HH# | e | 99 |
| Deliver the goods / *Liefere die Ware!* | 1942 | P378 | HM | | 99 |
| On thinking about Hell / *Nachdenkend, wie ich höre* | 1941 | P367 | NJ | | 100 |
| Summer 1942 / *Sommer 1942* | 1942 | P379 | MH | | 101 |
| The fishing-tackle / *Das Fischgerät* | 1943 | P386 | LB | | 101 |
| Five Hollywood elegies / *Fünf Hollywoodelegien* | 1942 | P380 | JW | e | 102 |
| The last elegy / *Die letzte Elegie* | 1942 | P381 | JW | e | 103 |
| The swamp / *Der Sumpf* | 1942 | P381 | NR | e | 103 |
| I, the survivor / *Ich, der Überlebende* | 1942 | P392 | JW | | 104 |
| **THEATRE AFTER 1945** | | | | | |
| Prologue to Galileo / *Prolog zur amerikanischen Aufführung* | ?1947 | PSP157 | JW | | 104 |
| Light as though never touching the floor / *Leicht, als ob nie den Boden berührend* | 1945 | P394 | MH | | 105 |
| The friends / *Die Freunde* | 1948 | P415 | MH | | 105 |
| The lighting / *Die Beleuchtung* | ?1951 | P426 | JW | | 105 |
| The curtains / *Die Vorhänge* | 1951 | P425 | JW | | 106 |
| Weigel's props / *Die Requisiten der Weigel* | 1950 | P427 | JW | | 107 |
| **FREEDOM AND DEMOCRACY** | | | | | |
| The anachronistic procession / *Der anachronistische Zug* | 1947 | P409 | JW | d | 108 |
| **THE FRESH START** | | | | | |
| Homecoming / *Die Rückkehr* | 1943 | P392 | JW# | e | 114 |
| War has been given a bad name / *Der Krieg ist geschändet worden* | 1945 | P403 | JW | | 114 |
| Encounter with the poet Auden / *Begegnung mit dem Dichter Auden* | ?1950/1 | P418 | JW | | 115 |
| Bad times / *Schlechte Zeiten* | 1949 | P416 | CM | | 115 |
| Observation / *Wahrnehmung* | 1949 | P415 | ME | | 116 |
| Love songs / *Liebeslieder* | 1950 | P429 BF15.452 | LL | d | 116 |
| **BUCKOW 1953, THE SHAKE-UP** | | | | | |
| The solution / *Die Lösung* | 1953 | P440 | DB | | 118 |
| Changing the wheel / *Der Radwechsel* | 1953 | P439 | MH | | 118 |
| Nasty morning / *Böser Morgen* | 1953 | P440 | DB | | 119 |
| Still at it / *Gewohnheiten, noch immer* | 1953 | P441 | DB | | 119 |
| Hot day / *Heisser Tag* | 1953 | P441 | DB | | 119 |

| Title | Date | Refs | Trs | Music | Page |
|---|---|---|---|---|---|
| The smoke / *Der Rauch* | 1953 | P442 | DB | m | 120 |
| Iron / *Eisen* | 1953 | P442 | AT | | 120 |
| The one-armed man in the undergrowth / *Der Einärmige im Gehölz* | 1953 | P442 | DB | | 120 |
| Eight years ago / *Vor acht Jahren* | 1953 | P443 | DB | | 121 |
| Reading Horace / *Beim Lesen des Horaz* | 1953 | P443 | MH | | 121 |
| This summer's sky / *Der Himmel dieses Sommers* | 1953 | P444 | MH | | 121 |
| The trowel / *Die Kelle* | 1953 | P445 | MH | | 121 |
| Reading a late Greek poet / *Bei der Lektüre eines spätgriechischen Dichters* | 1953 | P445 | MH | | 122 |
| The abandoned greenhouse / *Das Gewächshaus* | c.1954 | P448 | JW | | 122 |
| The little rose, oh how should it be listed? / *Ach, wie sollen wir die kleine Rose buchen* | 1954 | P447 | JW | | 123 |

RUSSIA REVIEWED

| Title | Date | Refs | Trs | Music | Page |
|---|---|---|---|---|---|
| Praise of the USSR / *Lob der UdSSR* | 1930 | PSP75 | JW | e | 123 |
| The Internationale / *Die Internationale* | 1932 | P202 | MM | | 124 |
| Washing / *Das Waschen* | 1937 | P290 BF14.642 | MH | | 125 |
| Is the people infallible? / *Ist das Volk unfehlbar?* | 1939 | P331 | JW | | 125 |
| The weights on the scales / *Die Gewichte auf der Waage* | 1956 | BF15.301 | JW | | 127 |
| The god is worm-eaten / *Der Gott ist madig* | 1956 | BF15.301 | JW | | 128 |
| Developing a wheat to stand the winter / *Zur Züchtung winterfesten Weizens* | 1956 | BF15.301 | JW | | 128 |
| Pride / *Stolz* | 1945 | P402 | HM | | 128 |

THIRTY YEARS OF GERMANY

| Title | Date | Refs | Trs | Music | Page |
|---|---|---|---|---|---|
| Germany, you blond pale creature / *Deutschland, du Blondes, Bleiches* | 1920 | P57 | CM | | 129 |
| O Germany, pale mother / *O Deutschland, bleiche Mutter* | 1933 | P218 | JW | | 130 |
| On Germany / *Über Deutschland* | 1939 | P346 | MH | | 131 |
| Germany (One stormy night) / *Deutschland* | 1942 | BF15.358 | JW# | d, e | 132 |
| Germany 1945 / *Deutschland / Im Haus ist der Pesttod* | 1945 | P404 | JW | | 132 |
| Children's anthem / *Kinderhymne* | 1950 | P423 BF12.442 | ER | e | 132 |

| Title | Date | Refs | Trs | Music | Page |
|---|---|---|---|---|---|
| Germany 1952 / *Deutschland 1952* | 1952 | P432 BF15.467 | JW | | 133 |
| **LIFE AND DEATH** | | | | | |
| Everything changes / *Alles wandelt sich* | c.1944 | P400 | JW | m | 133 |
| Once / *Einst* | 1945 | P404 | JW | | 134 |
| Only a fleeting glance / *Ach, nur der flüchtige Blick* | 1941/2 | P447 | JW | | 134 |
| When in my white room at the Charité / *Als ich im weissen Krankenzimmer der Charité* | 1956 | P451 | MH | | 135 |
| And I always thought / *Und ich dachte immer* | c.1955 | P452 | JW | | 135 |
| To those born later / *An die Nachgeborenen* | 1934–8 | P318 | # | e | 136 |

## KEY TO THE TRANSLATORS

| | | | | |
|---|---|---|---|---|
| EA | Edith Anderson | | CM | Christopher Middleton |
| WHA | W. H. Auden | | HM | Humphrey Milnes |
| LB | Lee Baxandall | | MM | Michael Morley |
| DB | Derek Bowman | | PLP | Patty Lee Parmalee |
| ME | Martin Esslin | | NR | Naomi Replansky |
| MH | Michael Hamburger | | ER | Edith Roseveare |
| EH | Elisabeth Hauptmann | | WR | William Rowlinson |
| HH | H. R. Hays | | SS | Stephen Spender |
| NJ | Nicholas Jacobs | | MS | Martin Sutton |
| FJ | Frank Jellinek | | AT | Antony Tatlow |
| LL | Lesley Lendrum | | JW | John Willett |

## EDITORIAL NOTES (* = new note † = additional note)

*Legend of the dead soldier*. Refers to the First World War. 'Kaiser' = the Emperor William II.

*The second psalm*. Füssen = about 90km south of Augsburg; Passau = where the Danube enters Austria.

*\*Of François Villon*. In Brecht's typescript there are seven extra stanzas, omitted from the original publication of 1926.

*\*Ballad of Mazeppa*. GW 233, Ged. 1. In *Devotions* 1922–67. First published in *Berliner Börsen-Courier*, 8 July 1923. Byron and Victor Hugo had written about Mazeppa, a seventeenth-century Ukrainian adulterer; Liszt composed a 'symphonic poem'.

†*Of poor B.B.* Hitherto published in its revised version, as in P 107.

*\*Tercets on love*. Were published also in the programme of Reinhardt's Kurfürstendamm-Theater [1931/vol. 6]. Notes in BF vol. 14 give an interesting account of Karl Kraus's commitment to this poem, originally titled 'The lovers'. They also mention its debt to a German translation of Dante's *Divine Comedy* [Canto 5 of the *Inferno*] and its citation as his favourite poem by Gottfried Benn in the anthology *Geliebte Verse* of 1951.

†*Song of the SA man.* Shortened by three stanzas from the version in Brecht: *Poems 1913–1956*, Methuen, London and New York, 1976. Music by Eisler in Brecht/Eisler: *Lieder Gedichte Chöre*, Paris, 1934.

†*The spring.* BF 14.527 introduces us to a shorter version, subsequent to the one used in the film *Kuhle Wampe.*

*\**But for the Jews advising against it.* Poem first published in *Gedichte aus dem Nachlass* (1982). There was a third stanza, which was not completed. It would have dealt with the rubbish believed by anti-semites, and runs:

> Everyone is aware that the multi-millionaire Karl Marx
> Together with Rothschild, the well-known bolshevik
> Drove Germany into the Franco-Prussian War; and was it not
> The Jew Abraham Lincoln, masquerading as an American President
> Who murdered the poet Schiller? And already it had been Charlemagne –
> Real name: Moritz Rosenthal – who sold the only
> Authentic Aryan to assume the Chinese imperial throne
> The famous Confucius, for thirty pieces of silver, or more precisely roubles
> To the Jewess Cleopatra, that gypsy whose real name was
> Sara Mayer.

†*The playwright's song.* When first published in 1956 the poem was headed 'fragment' and stopped at the end of the fourth section. The BF edition prints the remainder, from 'And so swiftly did the appearance' to the end, as a separate poem under the title 'Und so schnell wechselte zu meiner Zeit'.

†*Letter to the playwright Odets.* See Letter 288 to Victor J. Jerome, head of the agitprop section of the American Communist Party.

*\**The actress in exile.* Refers to Brecht's wife Helene Weigel in the Paris production of *Señora Carrar's Rifles* in October 1937. See his letter 341 to her, where he calls this poem 'one of the best things I've written about the art of acting'.

*\**An actress soliloquises while making up.* Written for his mistress Ruth Berlau, then playing an alcoholic in a Copenhagen production of Nordahl Grieg's play about the Paris Commune *The Defeat.*

†*Emigrant's lament.* The doctor is identified as Dr Waldemar Goldschmidt, who had been senior physician at the Vienna Rothschild-Krankenhaus and met Brecht in Sweden. See *Journal* entry for 7 November 1939.

†*Landscape of exile.* BF 15.356 says that the poem was dedicated to William Dieterle, the Hollywood producer and former Reinhardt actor who had helped the Brechts come to California. See Brecht's *Journal* entry for 9 August 1941. It seems likely to have been written around then, though Brecht signed the dedication two years later.

*\**The weights on the scales.* This and the two following poems were written by Brecht in July 1956, after he had received the proceedings of the Soviet Communist Party's Twentieth Congress at the end of June, with the text of Khrushchev's denunciation of Stalin and Stalinism five months earlier. The German texts were first published in 1989 in Brecht's *Gedichte aus dem Nachlass*, under a short note by Brecht to say 'At present there is no point in judging Stalin historically, and too few facts to make it worth trying. Nonetheless his authority must be demolished if the harmful effects of his example are to be swept away.'

*\**Germany (One stormy night).* One of a group of four songs that Eisler wrote for broadcasting to German prisoners of war in Russia. The second verse is based on Stalin's Army Order of 23 February 1942, which warned the troops against identifying Hitler's 'clique' with the German state. 'The experience of history tells us that Hitlers come and go, but the German people, the German state remains.' Brecht mentions the people only.

# Musical settings

This list gives settings by the principal composers who worked with Brecht – Kurt Weill, Hanns Eisler and Paul Dessau – together with melodies devised or annexed by the young Brecht, and a small number of those written by other composers, notably the short-lived Franz S. Bruinier who was his first professional musical collaborator. Most of its information has been derived from, or checked with, the invaluable catalogue by Joachim Lucchesi and Ronald Schull, *Musik bei Brecht*. Other sources include David Drew's *Kurt Weill: A handbook* and Manfred Grabs's Eisler catalogue.

Poem titles are given in order of appearance in the book, nearly always in German. If the title of the song setting differs it is also given, in brackets. Sometimes there is more than one version of a setting by the same composer; there may also be settings by more than one composer. The composer's name is given following the title. Numbers in the last column denote pages, unless otherwise indicated.

The following initials and abbreviations are used:

b  Bertolt Brecht
   HP  *Die Hauspostille* (Ullstein, Berlin 1927) and later editions, including the bilingual Brecht/Bentley: *Manual of Piety* (Grove Press, New York)

d  Paul Dessau (1894–1979)
   LuG  Brecht/Dessau: *Lieder und Gesänge* (Henschel-Verlag, Berlin 1957)
   MC  Brecht/Dessau: *Sieben Lieder zu Mutter Courage* (Lied der Zeit, Berlin 1949)

e  Hanns Eisler (1898–1962)
   EGW  Eisler: *Gesammelte Werke I/16. Lieder für eine Singstimme und Klavier* (Deutscher Verlag für Musik, Leipzig 1976)
   ELK  Eisler: *Lieder und Kantaten*. Ten volumes (Breitkopf & Härtel, Leipzig 1956–)
   Massnahme  Eisler: *Die Massnahme. Lehrstück*. KA (Universal-Edition, Vienna 1931)

m    Dominic Muldowney (1952–)
     DT   *In Dark Times* (Universal Edition, London 1980–1)
     5TP  *Five Theatre Poems* (Universal Edition, London 1980)
     X    *The Duration of Exile* (Universal Edition, London 1983)
w    Kurt Weill (1900–50)
     Piano scores (KA) of the following, published by Universal-
         Edition (Vienna) and European-American Music (New
         York) in various editions. Also individual songs and
         albums of songs from the works concerned:
     A&F  *Rise and Fall of the City of Mahagonny* (opera)
     DGO  *The Threepenny Opera*
     HE   *Happy End*
     KlM  *Mahagonny Songspiel*, or *Little Mahagonny*

     GBL  *Das grosse Brecht-Liederbuch* ed. Fritz Hennenberg.
         Three-volume selection from the above and other
         composers. Some piano accompaniments have been
         simplified (Suhrkamp, Frankfurt, and Henschel, Berlin
         1984)

| Page | Title | Composer | Publication |
|------|-------|----------|-------------|
| 4 | *Aus ist das Stück* (The play is over) | m | 5TP |
| 5 | *Legende vom toten Soldaten* | b | HP 156, GBL 8 |
|   |   | arr. Busch | GBL 10 |
| 12 | *Ballade von den Seeräubern* | arr. e | EGW 15 |
|   |   | b | HP 149, GBL 16 |
| 19 | *Ballade vom Weib und dem Soldaten* | b/Bruinier | GBL 44 |
|   |   | e | EGW 17, 20 |
|   |   | d | MC 8–15 |
| 22 | *Erinnerung an die Marie A.* | b | *Manual of Piety* |
|   |   | Bruinier | GBL 46 |
|   |   | b/Bruinier | GBL 42 |
|   |   | arr. e | EGW 25 |
| 26 | Alabama song | b | HP 153 |
|   |   | w | KlM |
| 27 | Mahagonny song no. 1 (*Auf nach Mahagonny!*) | w | KlM |
| 28 | Mahagonny song no. 3 (*Gott in Mahagonny*) | w | KlM |
| 30 | Benares song | b | HP 154 |
|   |   | w | KlM |
| 45 | *Terzinen über die Liebe* (Crane duet) | w | A&F sc. 14 |
| 46 | *Denn wie man sich bettet* (Jenny's song) | w | A&F sc. 16 |
| 47 | *Jenny, die Seeräuberbraut* (Pirate Jenny) | w | DGO sc. 2 |
| 48 | *Das Lied vom Surabaya-Johnny* | w | HE, GBL 106 |

| Page | Title | Composer | Publication |
|------|-------|----------|-------------|
| 50 | Das Lied von Mandelay | w | HE, GBL 102 |
| 51 | Die Ballade von der sexuellen Hörigkeit | w | DGO sc. 4 |
| 53 | Die Zuhälterballade (Tango-Ballade) | w | DGO sc. 7, GBL 72 |
| 54 | Der Kanonensong | w | DGO sc. 2, GBL 60 |
| 55 | Die Moritat vom Mackie Messer (Mac the Knife) | w | DGO, GBL 51 |
| 56 | Zweites Dreigroschen-Finale (Wovon lebt der Mensch?) | w | DGO sc. 6 |
| 59 | Lied von der belebenden Wirkung des Geldes | e | EGW4, 24, ELK1 140, 147, GBL 142 |
| 60 | Die Ballade vom angenehmen Leben | w | DGO sc. 6, GBL 75 |
| 61 | Neue Schlussstrophen | w | DGO film |
| 62 | Das Lied vom SA-Mann | e | EGW 17, 20, ELK5 53 |
| 63 | Ändere die Welt, sie braucht es | e | Massnahme Nr 9, EGW 23, ELK2 2 |
| 63 | Lob der Partei | e | Massnahme Nr 10 |
| 64 | Das Frühjahr kommt | e | EGW 22, ELK2 153 |
| 67 | Ballade von der 'Judenhure' Marie Sanders | e | EGW 17, 20, ELK2 37 |
| 75 | Der Nachschlag (The moment before impact) | m | 5TP |
| 80 | Finnische Landschaft | e | EGW 80, ELK1 26 |
| 86 | Auf den kleinen Radioapparat | e | EGW 78, ELK1 110, GBL 254 |
| 87 | Gedanken über die Dauer des Exils | e | EGW 53, ELK1 133 |
| 88 | Frühling 1938 | | |
| | (Ostersonntag) | e | EGW 91, ELK1 22 |
| | (Der Totenvogel) | e | EGW 79, ELK1 63 |
| 90 | Der Kirschdieb | e | EGW 93, ELK1 174, GBL 258 |
| 92 | Die Pfeifen (Auf der Flucht) | e | EGW 84, ELK1 76 |
| 92 | 1940 VI (Der Sohn) | e | EGW 75, ELK1 78 |
| 93 | Motto (Dies ist nun alles) | e | ELK2 90 |
| 94 | Mutter Courages Lied | d | MC 4, GBL 157 |
| 95 | Das Lied vom Rauch | d | LuG 76, GBL 168 |
| 96 | Über den Selbstmord | e | EGW 90 |
| | (In unserem Lande) | d | LuG 79 |
| | (On suicide) | m | DT |
| 97 | Das Lied von der Moldau | e | EGW 23, ELK8 68 |
| 97 | Ginge es in goldnen Schuhen | d | LuG 73 |
| 99 | Landschaft des Exils | e | EGW 154, ELK1 60 |
| 102 | Fünf Hollywoodelegien | e | EGW 105, ELK2 138 |
| 103 | Die letzte Elegie | e | EGW 102, ELK2 143 |
| 103 | The swamp (Der Sumpf) | e | EGW 113, ELK2 145 |
| 114 | Die Rückkehr (Die Heimkehr) | e | EGW 153, ELK1 38, GLB 264 |
| 116 | Vier Liebeslieder | d | GLB 308 |
| 120 | Der Rauch (The smoke) | m | X no. 4 |
| 123 | Lob der UdSSR | e | Massnahme Nr 2b, ELK2 114 |
| 132 | Deutschland (In Sturmesnacht) | e | EGW 17, ELK1 156 |
| 132 | Kinderhymne | e | EGW 21, ELK1 8 |
| 133 | Alles wandelt sich (Everything changes) | m | X no. 1 |

# Index of titles

Brecht's Plays, Poetry and Prose
*annotated and edited*
*by John Willett and Ralph Manheim*

**Collected Plays**

*The following plays are available in unannotated editions:*
The Days of the Commune; The Measures Taken and other
Lehrstücke; The Messingkauf Dialogues
*Also:* Happy End (by Brecht, Weill and Lane)

*\* in preparation*